Universal Design for Web
Applications

Other resources from O'Reilly

Related titles   Ambient Findability   Learning Web Design
                     Designing Web Navigation   Painting the Web
                     Information Architecture for   Website Optimization
                       the World Wide Web

oreilly.com   *oreilly.com* is more than a complete catalog of O'Reilly books. You'll also find links to news, events, articles, weblogs, sample chapters, and code examples.

oreillynet.com is the essential portal for developers interested in open and emerging technologies, including new platforms, programming languages, and operating systems.

Conferences   O'Reilly brings diverse innovators together to nurture the ideas that spark revolutionary industries. We specialize in documenting the latest tools and systems, translating the innovator's knowledge into useful skills for those in the trenches. Visit *conferences.oreilly.com* for our upcoming events.

Safari Bookshelf (*safari.oreilly.com*) is the premier online reference library for programmers and IT professionals. Conduct searches across more than 1,000 books. Subscribers can zero in on answers to time-critical questions in a matter of seconds. Read the books on your Bookshelf from cover to cover or simply flip to the page you need. Try it today for free.

Universal Design for Web Applications

Wendy Chisholm and Matt May

O'REILLY®

Beijing · Cambridge · Farnham · Köln · Sebastopol · Taipei · Tokyo

Universal Design for Web Applications
by Wendy Chisholm and Matt May

Published by O'Reilly Media, Inc., 1005 Gravenstein Highway North, Sebastopol,
CA 95472.

O'Reilly books may be purchased for educational, business, or sales promotional
use. Online editions are also available for most titles (*http://safari.oreilly.com*). For
more information, contact our corporate/institutional sales department: (800)
998-9938 or *corporate@oreilly.com*.

Editor: Simon St.Laurent
Production Editor: Loranah Dimant
Copyeditor: Loranah Dimant
Proofreader: Sada Preisch

Indexer: Ellen Troutman Zaig
Cover Designer: Karen Montgomery
Interior Designer: David Futato
Illustrator: Jessamyn Read

Printing History:
 November 2008: First Edition.

ISBN: 978-0-596-51873-8

[M]

1225997705

To my family, especially
John and Zeb

—Wendy

To Kristen and Rosalie

—Matt

Table of Contents

Preface

As you may have guessed, *Universal Design for Web Applications* addresses the architectural principle of universal design as applied to the Web. Practitioners of universal design are concerned with making their web content work as efficiently as possible across the range of capabilities exhibited by both people and their chosen browsing technologies.

The ultimate goal of universal design for the Web is to increase usability for people with disabilities and in scenarios involving mobile and embedded devices. As we discuss in Chapter 2, the proportion of web usage worldwide by means other than the desktop browser is increasing at an incredible rate, and users who have learned universal design practices are in the best position to design and maintain sites that meet those users' needs without returning to the bad old days of having to build one interface for every kind of browser.

Audience

Readers should be familiar with web page technology, particularly (X)HTML and CSS. There are separate chapters addressing JavaScript; Ajax and ARIA; and Rich Internet Applications in Flash, Flex, and Silverlight. If you don't use all of these technologies, feel free to skip those chapters.

This book should help:

- Web developers and designers who are looking to build universal design practices into their work
- Managers and trainers who are looking to help their organizations do the same
- Accessibility advocates looking for advice relevant to modern web design practices
- Anyone with web development or design skills who needs a refresher

How to Read This Book

This book is primarily built on the framework of the Web Content Accessibility Guidelines 2.0 (WCAG 2.0) and the Mobile Web Best Practices 1.0 (MWBP 1.0) produced by the World Wide Web Consortium. The information we have chosen to cover is primarily based on the Level A Success Criteria of the Web Content Accessibility Guidelines 2.0. This is not to say that the other levels are not important, but we assume most people will want to start somewhere and this is the best place to start—the minimum level of conformance. We strongly encourage you to look at the success criteria in the other levels and do as much as you can to address those.

However, this is not a WCAG 2.0 tutorial. We don't discuss how to claim conformance to WCAG 2.0. What we hope to achieve is a reference that helps the reader approach web design as we do—we hope you learn to ask some of the same questions that we ask, and make some of the same decisions. To that end, we have organized the book to focus on the process of design, and chapters are based on types of information—forms, document structure, and scripting.

We've also included a series of questions and show you how each maps to WCAG 2.0 and MWBP 1.0 and where to find more information about that particular topic within the book.

Where possible, we also point you to related references, such as the Authoring Tool Accessibility Guidelines 2.0 (ATAG 2.0), articles about universal design from the DO-IT program at the University of Washington, Internationalization Techniques, User Agent Accessibility Guidelines, and the Section 508 standards.

A Chapter Breakdown

Following is a detailed breakdown of the Table of Contents, including a brief description of what's covered in each chapter.

Chapter 1, *Introducing Universal Design*
Our take on universal design and how it applies to the Web, accessibility, and the mobile market.

Chapter 2, *Selling It*
How to convince your boss (or yourself) that universal design is imperative to the success of your website.

Chapter 3, *Metadata*
The story of the building blocks of universal design; information on alt text, long descriptions, labels, document-level language and encoding, and link text.

Chapter 4, *Structure and Design*
What you need to know about HTML and HTTP, including semantic markup, the use of color, style, web-friendly fonts, avoiding flicker, and designing for HTML-based email.

Chapter 5, *Forms*
How to use the features of HTML to design full-featured and usable forms; tab order, error handling on both client and server side, and the problems with CAPTCHA are covered.

Chapter 6, *Tabular Data*
How to mark up tables with the information necessary for users of all stripes to navigate them effectively.

Chapter 7, *Video and Audio*
A history of video on the Web, including support for different formats across device classes; and HOW-TOs for captioning, audio description, and transcription.

Chapter 8, *Scripting*
The keys to building JavaScript into web applications: progressive enhancement, unobtrusive script, and proper use of events.

Chapter 9, *Ajax and WAI-ARIA*
An introduction to accessibility for Ajax-based applications, including the basics of the W3C/WAI Accessible Rich Internet Applications (ARIA) specification.

Chapter 10, *Rich Internet Applications*
Universal design practices for Flash, Flex, and Silverlight.

Chapter 11, *The Process*
Tips on integrating universal design processes into the workflows of organizations of any size.

Conventions Used in This Book

The following typographical conventions are used in this book:

Constant width

> Indicates command-line elements, computer output, and code examples

Constant width italic

> Indicates variables in examples and registry keys

Constant width bold

> Indicates user input

Italic

> Introduces new terms and indicates URLs, commands, file extensions, filenames, directory or folder names, and UNC pathnames

 Indicates a tip, suggestion, or general note.

Indicates a warning or caution.

Using Code Examples

This book is here to help you get your job done. In general, you may use the code in this book in your programs and documentation. You do not need to contact us for permission unless you're reproducing a significant portion of the code. For example, writing a program that uses several chunks of code from this book does not require permission. Selling or distributing a CD-ROM of examples from O'Reilly books does require permission. Answering a question by citing this book and quoting example code does not require permission. Incorporating a significant amount of example code from this book into your product's documentation does require permission.

We appreciate, but do not require, attribution. An attribution usually includes the title, author, publisher, and ISBN. For example: "*Universal Design for Web Applications*, by Wendy Chisholm and Matt May. Copyright 2009 Wendy Chisholm and Matthew May, 978-0-596-51873-8."

If you feel your use of code examples falls outside fair use or the permission given above, feel free to contact us at *permissions@oreilly.com*.

Safari® Books Online

When you see a Safari® Books Online icon on the cover of your favorite technology book, that means the book is available online through the O'Reilly Network Safari Bookshelf.

Safari offers a solution that's better than e-books. It's a virtual library that lets you easily search thousands of top tech books, cut and paste code samples, download chapters, and find quick answers when you need the most accurate, current information. Try it for free at *http://safari.oreilly.com.*

How to Contact Us

We have tested and verified the information in this book to the best of our ability, but you might find that features have changed (or even that we have made mistakes!). Please let us know about any errors you find, as well as your suggestions for future editions, by writing to:

O'Reilly Media, Inc.
1005 Gravenstein Highway North
Sebastopol, CA 95472
800-998-9938 (in the United States or Canada)
707-829-0515 (international/local)
707-829-0104 (fax)

To ask technical questions or comment on the book, send email to:

bookquestions@oreilly.com

We have a web page for this book where we list examples and any plans for future editions. You can access this information at:

http://www.oreilly.com/catalog/9780596518738

The authors also have a website for this book at:

http://ud4wa.com/

For more information about books, conferences, Resource Centers, and the O'Reilly Network, see the O'Reilly website at:

http://www.oreilly.com

Acknowledgments

We both were privileged to work at the World Wide Web Consortium in the Web Accessibility Initiative (WAI). We've worked with hundreds of people around the world—all of whom are working to make the Web accessible to everyone. There are very few new ideas in this book; others have already documented most of these techniques. Our hope is to bring them together in one easy-to-use place. As such, this book references the work of many people and to them we give our thanks, in particular: Tim Berners-Lee, inventor of the Web, director of the W3C, and an all-around amazing dude; Judy Brewer, the director of the WAI; the chairs and participants of the various WAI Working Groups; and the staff and members of the W3C.

We owe a debt of gratitude to the late Dr. John Slatin, both for his qualities as a community leader and as a friend. The John Slatin Fund Accessibility Project was set up to help cover John's remaining medical bills by connecting organizations with accessibility experts (*http://www.knowbility.org/business/john -slatin/*). We encourage you to contribute in any way that you can.

A round of applause for our technical reviewers: Brian Fling, Andrew Kirkpatrick, Gez Lemon, Anitra Pavka, and Terrill Thompson. Thanks to Shawn Henry and Ryan Turner for their feedback on the introductory and process chapters and to Aaron Leventhal for schooling us in WAI-ARIA.

This book would not be possible without our editor, Simon St.Laurent.

Wendy's Acknowledgments

I would like to thank Sheryl Burgstahler, William Loughborough, Gregg Vanderheiden, Neal Ewers, Ben Caldwell, Mark Novak, the participants in the WCAG WG (1997–2006), Shawn Henry, Len Kasday, Sadee Whip, and the crew of caregivers who hung out with Zeb while I wrote (Cosmopolitan Kids, Hillary, Dalillah, Lori, Molly and Mary, Kristen, and Molly).

Matt's Acknowledgments

I would like to thank Andrew Kirkpatrick, Donna Kolnes, Al Gilman, Jutta Treviranus, Jan Richards, Jon Gunderson, Bob Regan, Jeffrey Zeldman, Molly Holzschlag, James Craig, and everyone on the WaSP Accessibility Task Force.

CHAPTER 1

Introducing Universal Design

There's a popular, and probably apocryphal, story that features a naval officer (sometimes it's a businessman) who receives a performance review that reads: "This officer never makes the same mistake twice. However, he appears to be attempting to make them all once."

Over the life span of the Web, we've learned a lot about what not to do. Sometimes, this trail of "don'ts" leads us in the direction of the "do." But all too often, another "don't" is lurking around the corner. Because of all of the complexities involved with heterogeneous servers and protocols and languages and authoring tools and browsers—and don't get us started about the *users*—we as web tradespeople are all too happy to give up on finding the *right* way to build our content, once we've found *some* way to build it.

Before web production can grow into a profession, we first need a science, a calculus—or at least, some kind of broadly applicable line of reasoning on which we can rely to keep the don'ts at bay. In this book, we put all those pieces together, to help ensure that we don't all keep making the same, or worst of all, self-perpetuating mistakes.

If our job is to create a science, we'll need to determine the core value against which we measure all our progress. In the past, many have advocated adherence to a technical standard—say, HTML—and we agree that web standards are important. (You should expect as much from two alumni of the World Wide Web Consortium, which has published nearly all of those standards.)

Still, adherence to a technical document does not a profession make. It's still possible to code oneself into a corner in fluent HTML. Real expertise comes from people who use their code and content to anticipate problems before they arise and to improve the user experience wherever they can.

For the purposes of this book, we will approach every problem we face with the ultimate goal of providing the greatest benefit to the greatest number of people possible. This is the principle of universal design (UD).

The field of UD grew out of disciplines where exclusion is common, and the consequences of that exclusion can be dramatic. We are specialists in one of those disciplines: accessibility to users with disabilities. People with disabilities often represent the most compelling cases for inclusive design—not just in information technology but also in the physical world. However, UD encompasses all possible contingencies involved in the design of an object or experience, whether they are physical, cognitive, economic, geographic, ergonomic, or even something as simple as user choice.

Ron Mace, an architect who dedicated much of his career to designing a more usable world, coined the term:

> Universal design is the design of products and environments to be usable by all people, to the greatest extent possible, without the need for adaptation or specialized design.

Over the years, we've found that web practitioners tend to discover an affinity for architecture. Matt, for one, has taken more photos of buildings over the years than he has of people. Conversations in some web design circles are as likely to gravitate toward names like Frank Gehry or Santiago Calatrava as they are to Tim Berners-Lee or Eric Meyer. We have come to recognize that it is because, like them, we deal with architecture every day. Although our failed designs rarely result in a physical catastrophe, we do make decisions that affect people's ability to navigate, interact, and seek and participate in communities of their own. Our architecture in many ways is their architecture—and so, we have a lot to learn from their rules and rigors. This book is our attempt to apply the architectural field of UD to the Web.

One of the biggest opportunities for universal design to take hold on the Web is with something you probably already own: a mobile phone. It is estimated that mobile devices will overtake computers as the method of accessing web content within the next few years, if they haven't already. As this transition takes shape, all of the contingencies we just outlined will play a role in how a piece of content is designed.

You will find that we come back to mobile and accessibility as our criteria throughout the book. This is not at all accidental. Between these two issues, we find concrete examples of nearly every kind of eventuality that will arise when humans come into contact with web content. We have concrete guidance to offer in order to make today's web content work better for both user groups because the techniques for making web applications work on mobile devices overlap so often with the techniques used to make content accessible to people with disabilities.

Mobile and accessible design are also at opposite ends of the spectrum when it comes to meeting our stated goal: while good mobile design has the potential to reach the greatest number—perhaps billions of people—accessible design practices can mean the difference between participating in many of the most basic life activities and being marginalized. It is a stunning example of the greater good.

Accessible Design: A Story

Even today, many grocery stores have a phone-in service, allowing people to place their orders and have a clerk gather the items for customer pickup. For someone who is blind, or who uses a wheelchair, or who can't lift heavy items, a service like this allows them to live unassisted. Those of us without these disabilities tend to think of things like grocery shopping as a chore, but it is so much more to those who can't do it themselves.

In 1998, Matt was a web developer at an online grocery delivery service based in the Seattle area. When users who were blind started calling in, there was little that was known about making the web usable for them. At the time, and unbeknownst to Matt, Wendy was working on what would later become the first Web Content Accessibility Guidelines. But the most official accessibility policy in the U.S. in 1998 was an amendment to the Rehabilitation Act of 1973 called Section 508, which requires federal agencies to make or purchase electronic and information technology that is accessible to people with disabilities.

Standards aside, one thing was clear: while for the soccer moms of the Puget Sound an online grocer was a convenient service, for people with disabilities it was life-enabling technology.

Accessibility to people with disabilities has always been tough to sell on its merits, however noble and intuitive they may be. The stereotypes and stigmas attached to disabilities and people with them are all deeply ingrained in our culture. The sad fact is that even in 2008, in spite of an array of assistive technologies that enable people who are blind to be equal members of the workforce, the National Federation of the Blind reports that the unemployment rate among people who are working age and legally blind in the U.S. is approximately 70%.

Think about that. 7 in 10. Regardless of your position on the political spectrum, this should not only alarm you but also motivate you to work toward increasing access to information, community, and, most critically, work and greater independence not only for people who are legally blind but anyone who has a disability.

Those of us who are passionate about accessibility are aware that continuing to ignore the design factors that create barriers only magnifies the problem. It is not a coincidence that the name of the leading screen reader, JAWS, stands for Job Access With Speech. Assistive technology, such as screen reader software, depends on machine-processable information—including names, descriptions, roles and states of objects, as well as the relationships between objects—which are not strictly necessary to create a visual user interface, Web or otherwise. This is why we must consider these needs in the everyday work we do.

On the other hand, the landscape for web design is changing for everyone. Since June of 2007, one device alone has driven a new, global awareness of designing for mobile devices. And it is rapidly enveloping us all.

When it comes to attracting users, the iPhone is an international phenomenon. Available in a growing number of countries, it appeals to early adopters—a common trait of Apple products—but also to people who prefer simple ways of getting things done. On July 11, 2008, the geeks and the seekers waited in line for hours to get one of the first iPhone 3Gs. To many of them, this was their own version of life-enabling technology. And woe to those who didn't understand the iPhone craze: at a store opening in the Los Angeles area, a reporter for KTLA descended on the crowd to poke the poor captive audience with a proverbial stick, and found himself a hair's breadth from being eviscerated.

It's easy to dismiss any discussion of the iPhone's impact on mobile computing as Apple fanaticism, but two features have undeniably altered the landscape:

- A mobile browser with desktop-like functionality
- A large user base with unmetered wireless access to the Web

Before the mobile Safari browser, the Web was a very different, very constrained experience. Users found the sites their carriers wanted them to find, thanks to the walled gardens constructed for them, and avoided straying too far for fear of outrageous bandwidth overage charges. But today, not only do millions use the iPhone for web access (some 94% of iPhone users, according to Apple, access the Web from their device), but full browsing applications have appeared on other platforms, and the possibility of returning to the tiny screens and minimum capabilities of the mobile Web of just a couple years ago already seems rather quaint. Furthermore, the market has spoken, and it doesn't want that mobile Web; it wants the Web that it has today, on any device, in any place. We know the market does not take no for an answer.

The web's post-hoc adaptation to mobile modes of interaction is not limited to phones, either. More and more portable electronics are coming equipped with wireless connectivity and embedded browsers: at least 71 million Nintendo DS systems and 38 million PlayStation Portables have been sold as of June 2008, and each one is Wi-Fi–equipped, as are instant-messaging devices like the Sony mylo. Amazon's Kindle e-book reader (which you may even be using to read this book) lets users get connected using a basic browser on the device's data service. And Nokia's N800 series Internet Tablets come complete with a full Mozilla-based browser, as well as the Adobe Flash 9 plug-in, all on an 800x480 display. The range of devices accessing the Web in the next few years will include both upgraded versions of the electronics we use today, and hundreds, perhaps thousands of new gadgets we haven't yet imagined.

In fact, not only will the number of non-PC Internet-connected devices pass that of Internet-connected PCs—on a global scale, it won't even be close. In 2007, Lee Kai-fu, the president of Google's China operation, said, "most Chinese users who touch the mobile Internet will have no PC at all." And the numbers prove it: according to a September 4, 2008 article in *The Economist,*[*] 29% of China's Internet users, or 73 million people, use the mobile Web—a 45% increase in the first half of 2008 alone. The article goes on to outline the efforts of the BRIC countries (Brazil, Russia, India, and China) not only to modernize their mobile and Internet infrastructures but to use new technology to leapfrog those of us in the so-called industrialized world. It's no coincidence that Google has invested heavily in creating a mobile platform called Android, or that Nokia has bought and committed the Symbian mobile OS to the open source world. All those new toys have to run something. And the web-browsing tech in nearly all of them will be more like a desktop browser than the comparatively slim mobile pickings of the last few years. For its part, Google has announced that the rendering engine behind Chrome, the browser it released in September 2008, will be in Android devices as well.

That isn't to say that this change will be without compromise. Let's look at the iPhone as an example. The iPhone's 480x320 display is just over 1/12 the resolution of a standard 1280x1024 monitor. Enabling the desktop-like experience on a screen that small requires the ability to zoom. Links are often hard to tap on with your finger because they are too small or too close together. (One critic has said it is like "clicking on a 20-pixel image with your 40-pixel finger.") And text entry, while arguably improved over competing phones' chiclet QWERTY keyboards, is still at best a third as efficient as a full keyboard.

---

[*] *http://www.economist.com/science/tq/displaystory.cfm?story_id=11999307*

It is here that we see the nexus between mobile interaction and disability. People with low vision use screen magnifiers in much the same way iPhone users stretch and pinch their way around the browser. People with fine-motor disabilities often have trouble using a mouse to navigate web pages because links are too small or too close together. Some people with more profound motor disabilities, such as cerebral palsy, use onscreen keyboards to enter text on sites—and they don't like having to type any more than most people using their mobile devices do.

It could be that the current crop of mobile device users is the best thing to happen to people with disabilities for a long time. When else have millions of people stood in line with $199 or €129 or £99 in hand to purchase a functional disability? Where people with disabilities have long been treated as a weak force in the market, mobile users are now dominating, and by winning themselves some concessions from websites in their thrall, maybe, just maybe, they have the potential to enable those whose needs run far deeper than mere convenience.

Putting Universal Design to Work

The silver lining to this design approach can best be described with a little more history. In 2000, that online grocery site Matt was working on finally realized that its monolithic approach to the user experience was not going to succeed. The more features that were piled on, the more unwieldy the core of the experience—find item, add to cart, check out—became. When users woke up one morning to an entirely different experience as the result of a merger, they lost all they had learned, causing them to lose patience and interest as well.

At the same time, people had begun to ask about using the site via their mobile devices, over the primitive WAP, a protocol that displayed "decks" of content one screen at a time, on devices that could usually handle only four lines at a time. With a site that relied all too heavily on JavaScript, frames, and layout tables, there was nothing there that could be repurposed to enable other devices to do anything useful on the site.

And yet, even back in 2000, it was possible to practice universal design. It all started by taking each user action and breaking it down into atomic tasks that took place in a determinable order. Beginning with these basic building blocks, it was possible to reconstruct the entire online grocery site in line with each of these tasks. The product was a simple site that used standard HTML, textual links for every action, and basic HTTP requests for each interaction with the server.

Using this as a starting point, any kind of user experience was possible. The core site worked with screen readers, as well as the first generation of mobile phones that supported HTML. Using the strategy of progressive enhancement, which we will discuss later, it was possible to create the same experience for existing customers, more cleanly and more quickly, while giving them the same look and feel they had before. A focus on universal design is what allowed us to stop working *around* HTML and start working *with* it.

CHAPTER 2

Selling It

The lights come up. You and your friends get up from your seats, shifting the popcorn tubs and candy boxes underfoot, and the discussion begins.

"That was amazing! I loved how the director was faithful to the novel it was based on."

"Yes. And I thought the ending tied all of the subplots together nicely."

You stand there, silently. You didn't get it. At all.

In fact, you look around at the others filing out of the theater, and the ruffled brows and other quizzical expressions you see indicate that maybe your friends are the only ones clued in to this particular masterpiece. You're inclined to shout out, "Did anyone else understand what just happened here?" But saying so would expose you as no more than a cola-slushy-slurping Neanderthal, forever doomed to scour IMDB for explications of any film more challenging than *Dumb and Dumber*. Instead, you say nothing. On the way home, you imagine that the director had stopped the film and explained it to your cohorts while you had stepped out for your ritual mid-film butter reload. You are searching for a way to prove to yourself that you are not as stupid as you were just made to feel.

No one likes feeling dumb, or being left out. But on some level, at some time, each of us has a barrier to overcome. This barrier can have its basis in your ambient environment, or in your cultural or educational background, or in how your brain is wired. It may just be too little sleep—and too little coffee. However it happens, though, the last thing that will occur to you is that you have a disability. What you are wishing for in this moment is some way to help yourself to the context necessary for you to understand what's in front of you, unaided.

Only very rarely does a film capture the essence of a complex subject so well that people with film-school degrees and 24 column inches in the *Village Voice* celebrate them along with the everyday moviegoer. And do you know what reviewers call a movie, novel, or song that has achieved that kind of success?

They call it "accessible."

They call its appeal "universal."

There Is No "Them"

We have made the pitch for accessibility to a number of organizations, from corporations to government agencies to open source projects to disability advocacy groups themselves. We do it because we want everyone to be able to participate fully in the online world. We hope that by giving people responsible for web applications a deeper understanding of the problems, and some practical guidance, we can help more people use universal design effectively and therefore help more people participate in our changing society.

That's the idealized view, anyway. What we usually encounter is hesitancy, if not hostility, to the idea of increasing a site's accessibility. *Why should we fix the site for disabled users? We don't even have any disabled users!*

The principal obstacle to overcome in making the case for accessibility is the stigma associated with disability. Among decision-makers, the word "disability" conjures thoughts of people with dark sunglasses and canes, or wheelchairs, or other noticeable distinctions between "us" and "them."

The reality, however, is that there *is* no "us" and "them." People with disabilities are the largest minority group, and any one of us can become a member at any time—either through injury or illness or age.

Specific to the Web, the issue has become less about the human user and more about how we are accessing web content. A person using an iPhone, for example, deals with tiny text, links that are hard to activate with a finger, difficulty with text entry, and other environmental issues such as screen glare. But there they are, using the Web by the millions. While using an iPhone is a choice and disability is not, there is enough overlap in the techniques and shared experiences that we believe the following: *On the Web, the issues we talk about can apply to every one of us, sometime, somewhere, even if they aren't always a problem.*

Audience Characteristics

So when we talk about accessibility, we're really just talking about people who are blind, right?

Well, no. While people who can't see well or at all are at a distinct disadvantage using visual resources such as the Web, far more people encounter unintended design barriers. With the rise in popularity of web video, tens of millions of people who do not hear well or at all are missing out. Mouse-driven sites prevent keyboard-only users from operating web applications. Depending on the person or the situation in which she finds herself, or the device she has chosen to use, someone may be facing one of these issues or all of them. This is not black and white; people's capabilities are on a continuum and change throughout their lifetimes, perhaps even within a single day.

How can change happen so quickly? You start your day checking email on your laptop in the kitchen. As you walk to the bus stop, you get an update on your mobile device, and you craft an answer as the bus rattles its way through the city. By the time you reach your office, you have five more emails. In the first two hours of your day, you have seamlessly shifted between different operating systems, browsers, screen sizes, and resolutions. Your kinesthetic surroundings change constantly: family distractions in the kitchen, noises from the bus and fellow commuters, vibrations and bumps from the bus. Lighting changed: soft lighting in the kitchen, sunlight on the bus, and bright overhead fluorescents at work. You went from a trackpad on your laptop, to keyboard-only operation via your mobile, to a wireless mouse at your desk.

These changes represent the four categories of disabilities:

- Cognitive, reading, and learning
- Hearing
- Movement
- Vision

Table 2-1 provides a grossly oversimplified look at disabilities. For more information, the article "How People with Disabilities Use the Web" (*http://www .w3.org/WAI/EO/Drafts/PWD-Use-Web/Overview.html*) is a good place to start. It describes how different disabilities affect web accessibility, provides scenarios of people with disabilities using the Web, and outlines the variety of assistive technologies and adaptive strategies that people with disabilities use.

Table 2-1. Disability by class and situation[a]

Category	Includes (but is not limited to)...	Statistics	Situational
Cognitive, reading, and learning	Dyslexia, ADHD, low reading level	ADHD—4.4% of adults	Search engines (low-level interpretation of meaning), international or young readers
Hearing	Hard of hearing, deafness	Deafness—421,000 in both ears Hard of hearing—36.4 million with "hearing trouble"	Riding a packed train while listening through ill-fitting earphones, watching TV in a pub with the sound off
Movement	Paralysis, tremor, missing or loss of limb, weakness	2.5 million can't "grasp or handle small objects"	With an iPhone, your 40–80-pixel finger has difficulty accurately selecting 20-pixel links
Vision	Low vision, blindness, colorblindness	14.1 million people with "vision trouble" (includes colorblindness) 1.3 million people are legally blind	Screen magnification on an iPhone/iPod touch

[a] Statistics are estimates and U.S.-based. Sources: CDC Viral and Health Statistics Series 10, Number 232, Dec. 2006 (vision trouble, hearing trouble, adult ADHD, grasp/handle objects); AFB (legally blind); Gallaudet, *http://gri.gallaudet.edu/Demographics/factsheet.html#Q3* (deaf in both ears).

It is also important to to consider *situational disabilities*—changes in one's abilities based on environment, device, or other temporary conditions. Consider the following:

Mobile
> Hearing, motor, vision

International
> Reading

Search engines
> Cognitive, hearing, vision

Also consider that disabilities increase with age: 2.7% of Americans between 5–17 years old have disabilities compared with 41.4% of people 65 and older.

Configurability

The variations among your users are increasing. We are living longer and starting to use computers younger and younger. (Wendy's two-year-old even has a favorite reading website that he likes to visit.) New devices coming to the market—the iPhone, of course, and other mobile devices and platforms, as well as tiny laptops, such as the Eee PC—are changing how people see the Web. We're accessing information in more situations—while we're cleaning the house or working out. The variety of languages and cultures accessing the Web is growing. Bandwidth varies from dial-up (yes, even in the U.S.) to countries that are starting with mobile networks (Africa) to some mobile networks reaching broadband speeds. The interfaces that we use to connect and contribute to the Web are branching—short messaging service (SMS) is now as universal among the world's younger generations as radio, and mobile video is on the march.

The combinations of devices, preferences, and abilities are infinite. You may want to use information sightless even though you aren't blind. Your preferences may change throughout the day or from application to application—do you want voice input while you're writing a book, voice output while you're reading web pages, and a large-font visual display while you're reading email?

Challenge your assumptions about users. Don't assume that someone who is blind, for example, doesn't want to buy car insurance. We recently heard about a man who is blind who wanted to research car insurance for his wife. The site he tried to access assumed that because someone who is blind can't drive, he won't need to read about car insurance.

Growth Opportunity

As the Baby Boom generation ages, more and more people will face the challenges of reduced dexterity, vision, and hearing. So enabling accessible *technology* is a growth opportunity...[*]

—Steve Ballmer, 2001

Designing for a variety of situations and abilities can not only change your perspective, but it can also increase your audience. Consider how the world is changing and what that means for people. In 2000, the World Health Organization (WHO) estimated that 7–10% of the world's population (500 million people) live with a disability.[†]

---

[*] http://businessweek.com/bwdaily/dnflash/jun2001/nf20010613_081.htm

[†] http://www.who.int/inf-pr-2000/en/note2000-16.html

In the U.S., 1 in 5 people lives with a disability.[‡]

This number is expected to grow as people live longer—for example, predictions indicate that by 2011, people over 65 will make up 25% of Japan's population. According to the WHO, the fastest growing population group in industrial nations is the 80-and-over segment.[§]

There are two factors that tell us to pay attention to the number of older users on the Web. First, users in the 49–64 age group are coming online in increasing numbers, and with good reason: their stock portfolios, pay stubs, tax filing, and health-care information are now on the Web. These late-career workers are very attractive to marketers, particularly because "older" and "richer" are strongly correlated.

The second reason is that sooner or later, *they* are going to be *us*. We may be able to read 8-point text on our laptops today, but as we age, it's likely that that will become more difficult and we'll experience things such as headaches from squinting at that text. We may recognize that we're getting older, but what we will *say* is that the page we're using was poorly designed—and we'll be right. In fact, this is one of the problems with consigning features like magnification and high contrast to an accessibility link or control panel: people who are simply getting older don't think of themselves as disabled. You may know that your vision isn't 20/20 anymore, but why on earth would you look for solutions behind a picture of a wheelchair?

The beauty of universal design is in its capacity to enable everyone to use the same content according to their needs and wishes. *Universal design will help you reach more people and continue to reach them throughout their lives.*

Many devices "experience" limitations similar to those experienced by people with disabilities. In 2002, programmer Karsten Self declared that Google is a "blind user" in the sense that Google can only glean from a website that which can be programmatically determined—much the same way that a screen reader is limited (*http://zgp.org/pipermail/linux-elitists/2002-January/003912 .html*) . For both Google and screen readers, "text is king." Matt spun Karsten's statement for the current state of issues in accessibility:

> Google is, for all intents, a deaf user. A billionaire deaf user with tens of millions of friends, all of whom hang on his every word.[ǁ]
>
> —Bestkungfu Weblog, "Google is a deaf user"

[‡] 1997 Census Brief

[§] *http://www.who.int/mip/2003/other_documents/en/E%20AAE%20Towards%20Policy%20for %20Health%20and%20Ageing.pdf*

[ǁ] *http://www.bestkungfu.com/archive/date/2004/11/google-is-a-deaf-user/*

Universal design will increase the discoverability of your design.

Some situations create limitations that are similar to those experienced by people with disabilities. As we mentioned earlier, we call these situational disabilities. A small screen on a mobile device simulates the experience of someone using a screen magnifier (*http://www.w3.org/WAI/EO/Drafts/PWD-Use -Web/#screenmag*) on an average-size monitor—which is often said to be like looking at the page through a straw. A person using a kiosk in a shopping mall is surrounded by noise and unable to hear the audio of a presentation, simulating the experience of someone who is hard of hearing. A mechanic working on the underside of an airplane needs to access information without removing her hands or eyes from the task. And even the brightest, clearest mobile device displays are difficult to read in sunlight. *Designing for everyone will help you create content that more people can use in more situations.*

Legal Liability

> The Internet is a cornerstone of the modern economy. One of the country's largest retailers cannot exclude an entire segment of the population from its goods and services. This lawsuit is a warning to all large companies with an Internet presence that the blind will not be left behind on the information superhighway.#
>
> —From NFB v. Target Fact Sheet

Around the world, there are many international laws securing the rights of people with disabilities with respect to web content. In the U.S., these include the Rehabilitation Act Amendments of 1998, Section 508; the Americans with Disabilities Act (ADA) of 1990; and in the mobile space, Section 255 of the Telecommunications Act. All of these are in addition to various state-specific policies.

In the UK, the primary legislation is the Disability Discrimination Act 1995 (DDA). Unlike Section 508, the DDA applies to all websites, not just those that are government-funded.

At the time of this writing, the European Union (EU) does not have specific legislation, but several EU member states (including Germany, Spain, Italy, Ireland, and Portugal) have legal mandates for web accessibility. In addition, an agreement known as the Riga Declaration, signed unanimously by the EU, requires each member state to make its own governmental sites accessible by 2010.

Available at *http://dralegal.org/cases/private_business/nfb_v_target.php*

Australia, Canada, Israel, India, Japan, Korea, and New Zealand all have related policies. Visit *http://www.w3.org/WAI/Policy/* for more information.

As we write, some of these laws are being tested and others are being refreshed–strengthening their applicability to the Web with specific guidance for web applications.

One recent case is the National Federation of the Blind (NFB) versus Target Corporation. The NFB sued Target in a class action lawsuit on behalf of all Target customers in the United States who are blind and were unable to use the website before 2006. Early on in the case, Judge Marilyn Hall Patel rejected Target's position that their site couldn't be sued under the ADA because the services of *Target.com* were separate from Target's brick-and-mortar stores. The following is from her ruling on September 7, 2006:

> [T]he 'ordinary meaning' of the ADA's prohibition against discrimination in the enjoyment of goods, services, facilities or privileges, is that whatever goods or services the place provides, it cannot discriminate on the basis of disability in providing enjoyment of those goods and services.

Judge Patel also rejected Target's argument that its liability should be limited because it eventually made some improvements to its site. The key issue was whether, and how thoroughly, they responded to users' problems.

Target settled the case in August 2008. While not admitting any wrongdoing, the company did pay $6 million in damages to the plaintiffs. This does leave the question of the ADA's applicability to the Web somewhat unresolved. However, a settlement of that size is an eye-opener. Had Target simply worked in good faith to resolve the issues once the plaintiffs had approached them (in 2005), it could have spent a tiny fraction of the amount it did—5%, or $300,000, would have been more than enough. Instead, it'll give $40,000 a year to NFB for monitoring, on top of that $6 million payoff, all before it spends a dime on actual accessibility repair.

All that said, legal action is the last resort for accessibility advocates. A suit filed against a company is costly in terms of time, money, and goodwill. But in this day and age, wherever you are in the world, there is no excuse for discrimination.

For more information, refer to the NFB v. Target Fact Sheet at *http://dralegal .org/cases/private_business/nfb_v_target.php*.

The Standards

Industry standards will help you meet the laws. Especially now that WCAG 2.0 has been updated to address technologies such as Ajax, conforming to WCAG 2.0 will put you ahead of the game.

The World Wide Web Consortium (W3C) and the Web Accessibility Initiative (WAI)

Most of the standards covered in this book are products of the W3C,[*] in particular the WAI[†] whose purpose is to "[work] with organizations around the world to develop strategies, guidelines, and resources to help make the Web accessible to people with disabilities." The WAI wrote "Essential Components of Web Accessibility," which you can find at *http://www.w3.org/WAI/intro/components.php*, to explain how each of the components addressed by the separate guidelines is needed to make the Web accessible.

Web Content Accessibility Guidelines (WCAG)

> The Web Content Accessibility Guidelines (WCAG) documents explain how to make Web content accessible to people with disabilities. Web "content" generally refers to the information in a Web page or Web application, including text, images, forms, sounds, and such.
>
> —*http://www.w3.org/WAI/intro/wcag.php*

WCAG 1.0 was published as a W3C Recommendation in 1999. Since then it has been used as the basis for a variety of government and organizational policies around the world.

WCAG 2.0 has nearly emerged from the W3C process. At the time of this writing, its current status is "Proposed Recommendation." Assuming that the W3C membership supports this draft, which seems very likely, it will become a W3C Recommendation (i.e., "done") sometime in late 2008 or early 2009. This book references the November 3, 2008 Proposed Recommendation (*http://www.w3.org/TR/2008/PR-WCAG20-20081103/*). When in doubt, refer to the latest version of WCAG 2.0 at *http://www.w3.org/TR/WCAG20*.

The Web Content Accessibility Guidelines are developed by the Web Content Accessibility Guidelines Working Group (*http://www.w3.org/WAI/GL/*).

---

[*] Visit *http://www.w3.org/* for more about the W3C.

[†] Visit *http://www.w3.org/WAI/* for more about the WAI.

Authoring Tool Accessibility Guidelines (ATAG)

ATAG provides advice to developers of authoring tools, which broadly includes any tool that could be used to put content on the Web, such as HTML and XML editors, word processors, content management systems (CMSs), blogs, wikis, and social networking sites. The goals of ATAG are:

- Producing accessible output (that is, web pages) that meets standards and guidelines
- Prompting the content author (that is, the authoring tool user) for accessibility-related information
- Providing ways of checking and correcting inaccessible content
- Integrating accessibility in the overall "look and feel," help, and documentation
- Making the authoring tool itself accessible to people with disabilities

Visit *http://www.w3.org/WAI/intro/atag.php* for more information. The Authoring Tools Accessibility Guidelines Working Group develops ATAG. ATAG 1.0 became a W3C Recommendation in 2000. ATAG 2.0 is under development and will be compatible with WCAG 2.0.

User Agent Accessibility Guidelines (UAAG)

> The User Agent Accessibility Guidelines (UAAG) documents explain how to make user agents accessible to people with disabilities, particularly to increase accessibility to Web content. User agents include Web browsers, media players, and assistive technologies, which are software that some people with disabilities use in interacting with computers.
>
> —*http://www.w3.org/WAI/intro/uaag.php*

UAAG 1.0 was published as a W3C Recommendation in 2002. The first Working Draft of UAAG 2.0 was published in 2008—which means it has barely left the station on its trek through the W3C process.

The Accessible Rich Internet Applications Suite (WAI-ARIA)

> WAI-ARIA, the Accessible Rich Internet Applications Suite, defines a way to make Web content and Web applications more accessible to people with disabilities. It especially helps with dynamic content and advanced user interface controls developed with Ajax, HTML, JavaScript, and related technologies.
>
> —*http://www.w3.org/WAI/intro/aria.php*

Because this book focuses on web applications, we've devoted an entire chapter to ARIA (see Chapter 9), this exciting specification that seems on the fast track to W3C Recommendation. All of the major browsers have begun to support ARIA and a new wave of development and evaluation tools are appearing that can generate and check for its use. Assistive technologies are also beginning to support the richness ARIA offers.

Mobile Web Best Practices (MWBP)

> The principal objective is to improve the user experience of the Web when accessed from such devices.
>
> —*http://www.w3.org/TR/mobile-bp/*

The Mobile Web Best Practices 1.0 became a W3C Recommendation in July 2008. A related document that we often reference is the dotMobi Mobile Web Developer's Guide, which was built on the MWBP.

Professionalism

When making the case for a company to implement accessible design practices, it is possible that one approach may be more compatible than the others we discussed here. Businesspeople may not, for example, believe that there is a market to be gained by increasing accessibility. They may not (yet) care about mobile devices, or situational disabilities, or even the threat of legal action.

Fear not, good reader. There is another arrow in your quiver.

Corporations, with limited exceptions, exist to make a profit. And so, it would follow, doing more work on a fixed resource such as a website without a nexus to the profit motive is usually a nonstarter. What it takes in situations like these is an approach that solves an existing problem limiting efficiency in the organization. Today, one such problem is a lack of standards and best practices among professional web teams.

That's great, but where does universal design come in?

The ability to write valid code, separate structure and presentation, design for progressive enhancement, use technologies appropriately—these are the hallmarks of universal design.

As people develop their skills in standards-based design, they learn most of these practices, hone them on site after site, talk about their experiences, and keep learning. To practice universal design is to know not just *one* way to put something together but to know which of a number of possible solutions is the best.

If holes in a designer's skill set make him inflexible when it comes to building a website, that site will also lack flexibility, which would mean making changes would be more difficult. Redesigns get bogged down, and things tend to end up looking eerily similar to the way they did when they started. In more advanced cases of this particular disease, websites enter a kind of vapor lock, where changes stop happening because they take too much time, are too expensive, and generally cause headaches all around. This is not how to do business.

If you are nodding your head at these sentiments, chances are good that you need more professional web help. If you're the one in charge of hiring or contracting with web developers and designers, this part of the job is relatively easy: you use the power of the purse. When you're filling a position or putting out a request for quotes, mention standards-based design, accessibility, and mobile design explicitly.

There's one response you may hear from developers that should set off red flags. We have experienced individual developers, or even entire teams who object vociferously to spending time on universal design.

Sometimes their consternation is rooted in the idea of having to do work on something other than a feature. This is common in organizations that work on tight deadlines and with lots of people watching for progress. In situations like this, it's good to emphasize that a focus on universal design is a focus on quality, and you don't sacrifice quality in order to deliver more features.

The worst reason to hold up the process is to satisfy a prejudiced developer. Sadly, this is only too common. Read the comments on any Slashdot thread on accessibility, and you will find some of the most virulent antidisability commentary anywhere. You may never hear a complaint about making design tweaks for the iPhone. But suggest designing to address disabilities, and you could get an earful. Some of the gems we've heard:

- "We shouldn't have to design for blind users."
- "It's not our problem if screen readers can't deal with our content."
- "It's our right to decide who can and can't access our site."

It's at this point that all rational discussion ends.

We're going to skip the argument that people with disabilities are still people, though sometimes this needs reinforcing. Where you should be concerned as a stakeholder in this process is that comments like this show a lack of leadership. In this debate, you have implementers who are willing to ignore the needs of your potential users, risking goodwill and possibly legal liability, simply to avoid more work. What could you expect of someone like this when she is managing your engineering team? The software development process involves compromise—with management, customers, other business processes—legal compliance, and a host of other complications. Good managers know how to navigate these myriad issues with care. Can you trust those who would put their own prejudices to work to obstruct universal design with other important decisions?

Early and Often

Shawn Henry writes in her book *Just Ask: Integrating Accessibility Throughout Design* (*http://www.lulu.com*):

> When accessibility is considered early and throughout design, it can be seamlessly and elegantly integrated with overall product design. Incorporating accessibility early decreases the time and money to design accessible products and increases the positive impact that accessibility can have on design overall.

History has shown that products designed for universal access make services easier to use for everyone. Many watershed products were inspired by disability: the phone, the typewriter, speech recognition, optical character recognition (OCR), speech synthesis, and curb cuts.

Oftentimes, universal design and accessibility are one of the last things checked before a product ships, at which time they are usually put off until a future version or "bolted on" with predictably poor results.

When you don't include universal design early and often in a project, not only are you missing the opportunity to create an innovative product and increase your user base, you will likely spend 50–200 times more to retrofit the product than if you had included it in the project's specification.[‡]

Summary

"It is the stairs that make the building inaccessible, not the wheelchair."[§]

There are many cool (carrot) reasons to implement universal design: it's usually a great engineering problem (drawing on your creativity to solve architectural and design issues), it can increase your market (and make you more money), and it's the right thing to do. When the carrots fail to inspire, there are still many other reasons (sticks)—from business practicalities to protection against legal liability—that can be used to advocate the universal design approach.

[‡] Based on figures in McConnell, Steve. *Rapid Development: Taming Wild Software Schedules.* Microsoft Press (1996). as referenced in *http://en.wikipedia.org/wiki/Waterfall_model*.

[§] South African White Paper on an Integrated National Disability Strategy (*http://www.un.org/esa/socdev/enable/disberk2.htm*).

Universal design is innovative. It's fun. It's rewarding. So, what are you waiting for?

CHAPTER 3

Metadata

One person's content is another person's metadata.

—Stu Weibel

Among document formats, HTML is perhaps the most thoroughly researched with regard to accessibility. We know its strength is in its ability to express semantic meaning. In fact, most of HTML accessibility is about using semantics and structure correctly, enhancing them or working around their limitations.

When you look at your site, what do you see? Now load it in an older mobile device or mobile device emulator or a screen reader. Or find out what a search engine knows about it. The differences between your answer and theirs are the reason metadata is important.

What Is Metadata?

The typical definition of metadata is "data about data." Samantha Starmer recently explained (*http://tinyurl.com/6x5zve*) how we use metadata to make decisions every day. What *kind of* food do you want for lunch? What *color* shirt do you want to wear today? As humans, we constantly identify properties of objects, create labels for the properties, then categorize the objects based on the labels—it is some of the first language that we learn (as shown in Figure 3-1): round, square, red, blue, tall, short.

Why is metadata so important on the Web? Tags, labels, document structure, and descriptions help us sift through the heaps of information available online...and we're all contributing to it. In online communities, such as Flickr, Twitter, and Facebook, we use metadata to describe ourselves—our interests, our location, our likes and dislikes, and even our relationship status. This metadata helps us discover other people with similar interests. We can follow

Figure 3-1. A child's shape sorter toy; http://flickr.com/photos/ellasdad/425813314/

colleagues and visionaries to see what they are reading and watching, with whom they are talking, and what they are doing, potentially influencing decisions we make in our work and at play.

Universal design of metadata—as with other aspects of universal design—is about ensuring everyone can contribute their own metadata and also that we can all have access to the metadata that we need in order to make decisions.

In this chapter, we explore how search engines use metadata and how people with disabilities use it to find and navigate through content. Although we don't address how metadata is used in content adaptation, it is an important technique in learning environments and mobile situations. There is quite a lot of work in this area, including the IMS Access For All specification and the W3C Content Transformation Guidelines 1.0.

Images

In HTML, the `alt` attribute on the `img` element may be considered metadata for some; for others, it is *the* content. For images used as links or buttons, lack of metadata creates an insurmountable barrier to people using screen readers.

We (and here we mean the big "We"—accessibility advocates around the globe) have been talking about accompanying images with brief textual alternatives ("alt text") since September 1993, when Frans van Hoesel proposed the `alt` attribute, seven months after the first discussions of the `img` element (img: *http://1997.webhistory.org/www.lists/www-talk.1993q1/0182.html* and alt: *http://ksi.cpsc.ucalgary.ca/archives/WWW-TALK/www-talk-1993q3.messages/983.html*). Fifteen years later, images appear on almost every website but it's estimated that only 7% provide adequate alt text for images.[*] That's disappointing.

---

[*] *http://news.bbc.co.uk/2/hi/technology/6210068.stm*

So, folks are taking the issue into their own hands. Services such as WebVisum (*http://www.webvisum.com/*) are using optical character recognition (OCR) to ferret out the text within pictures of text (raster-based images). The technology is so good that it can solve CAPTCHAs—those twisty, hard-to-read words that are supposed to test whether you are human or a spambot trying to enter a site. Unfortunately, the primary test has become how well you can read twisty, hard-to-read words, creating a barrier for people who can't see or read well—until now.

This isn't to say that you are off the hook for providing alt text. People using screen readers are not the only ones looking at your alt text: search engines and mobile users need alt text, too.

As we noted in Chapter 2, Google is blind and deaf with tens of millions of friends and billions of dollars (and euros and yen...) to spend. The Google Webmaster Guidelines[†] recommend:

- Try to use text instead of images to display important names, content, or links. The Google crawler doesn't recognize text contained in images.
- Make sure that your TITLE tags and ALT attributes are descriptive and accurate.

Both the W3C's Mobile Web Best Practices (*http://www.w3.org/TR/mobile-bp/*) and the dotMobi Mobile Web Developers Guide (*http://dev.mobi/content/dotmobi-mobile-web-developers-guide*) say, "Provide an alt text value for images." Waiting for images to download and display can cost users money and time.

Keys to Writing Good Text Alternatives

Images are used for a variety of purposes, and therefore the requirements for writing the text alternatives depend on the purpose of the image. When penning a text alternative for an image, the first question you should ask yourself is, "What is the purpose of this image?" Is it a graph indicating sales growth of a product? Is it a button that links to the home page? Is it a webcam showing the current weather conditions on campus? Is it a test to determine if the entity interacting with your content is human or a spambot? Is it a piece of art? These are only a few situations in which you might be using a given image. We'll provide a few examples to help you consider how to write good text alternatives.

[†] *http://www.google.com/support/webmasters/bin/answer.py?answer=35769*

Figure 3-2. Photo by Rosalie Town in need of a description

Pictures of Recognizable Objects

Any change from nontext content to text involves some amount of signal loss. Your responsibility as an author is to compensate for that lost data as efficiently as possible. It may help to imagine describing the image you're seeing to someone on the phone. (Try it with lolcats: "It's this cat looking really surprised and unhappy, and the text says 'DO NOT WANT!'")

There is no right answer, strictly speaking, when it comes to alt text. Good alt text is situational and therefore subjective. For example, Figure 3-2 shows a picture.

How would you describe it? Perhaps something like:

```
alt="a mosque with five tall minarets, two of which are
under construction"
```

And nobody would fault you for that. You could probably get away with less, though "mosque" is a bit too terse.

Of course, we're cheating. We know the name of this mosque and where it's based. So we could refer to it canonically:

```
alt="the al-Saleh mosque in Sana'a, Yemen"
```

And if we were to use this in a blog post about the city, we might say:

```
alt="al-Saleh mosque viewed from al-Saba'in Park"
```

Any of these is an adequate alternative for most applications.

If you're teaching a class on architecture, though, a few words certainly do not do the photo justice. You would want your students to understand many, many details irrelevant to the casual reader. For example, al-Saleh's 6 minarets (including the one hidden in the photo) are each 328 feet tall. The central dome is 90 feet in diameter, and the main hall occupies over 146,000 square feet. The cream and beige look on the minarets is strongly evocative of the distinctive painted brick highlights found in the old city of Sana'a.

That's great information, but don't go shoving it all in the alt attribute. There's another attribute called longdesc, which is meant to point to long descriptions of the image. Create a file (say, *mosque-longdesc.html*), and point to it in the longdesc attribute:

```
<img alt="the al-Saleh mosque in Sana'a, Yemen"
longdesc="mosque-longdesc.html" />
```

 One of the most common pitfalls of longdesc is that authors will type the text of the description into the attribute value. Don't do this! The longdesc attribute always points to a URL.

Sadly, even after 11 years of longdesc, it's still not very well supported. To get around this, WCAG 1.0 suggested descriptive links (or "D-links," so named because it was determined that they should be text links that read "[D]"). It's an unattractive solution, and people who haven't discovered D-links before are unlikely to click on them. But where long descriptions are useful, many people still need them.

One way to break the logjam is with script. Here's one attempt to make longdesc useful to more people, using JavaScript to map the attribute value to the user interface of the image: *http://www.malform.no/acidlongdesctest/*.

Links

Alt text for images in links is somewhat different from that of regular images. The alt text we just described for the average image is usually a noun or some kind of representation of the image's content. But for links, it's a verb and represents where the link will take you. It may be a rounded green arrow pointing right, but if it links to the next page of an article, that's what it should say:

```
<a href="page2.html"><img src="rightarrow.gif" alt="next page" /></a>
```

Graphs

A graph—be it a pie chart or a 10,000-point histogram—is a visual represen-tation of a number of data points, usually organized to show a trend. Good alt text will describe the purpose of the graph:

```
alt="Acme stock chart"
```

Better alt text will briefly describe the trend:

```
alt="sunspot activity over the last two centuries follows a
consistent 11-year trend"
```

But the best you can do with multivariate data is to link to a table of the data from which the graph was constructed:

```
<a href="stocktable.html"><img src="stockchart.gif"
alt="view stock data" /></a>
```

Tabular data is covered in Chapter 6.

Logos

Logos are functional equivalents to company or product names. Again, don't stress over it. If it's a link, say where the link goes. If it's not, say what it is: a logo. And if you're talking about corporate branding (say, describing Coca-Cola's cursive logotype to a marketing class), make room for the long descriptions.

Webcams

If you're broadcasting an image from a webcam, which is updated on a regular interval, all you need to say is what you know will be true of that image. For example, there's a camera focused on the University of Washington campus quad known as Red Square, which could have alt text such as the following:

```
alt="Live picture of Red Square"
```

It's not necessary to go overboard describing the neo-Gothic façade of Suzzallo Library, the red brick plaza, the Gerberding Hall bell tower, the trees, or the fountain in the background. That's the kind of thing you'd use `longdesc` for. In this case, most people are probably just looking to see if it's raining. If you're intending for people to know what the weather is, or how many Jolt colas are left in the machine, you should provide some other way to access that infor-mation in parallel. But you don't know what is going to be happening at any given moment on the average live camera, so don't overthink it.

CAPTCHA

CAPTCHA images usually don't have alt text, as their entire existence is based around them not being programmatically readable. So the alt text that should go with a CAPTCHA is pretty simple:

```
alt="captcha"
```

However, you're not done. If you require your users to complete a CAPTCHA, you will have to provide users with some other way to accomplish the task that doesn't require the ability to cherry-pick text out of a distorted image.

Better yet, don't use them at all. We've already covered the fact that they're easily defeated, and their by-design inaccessibility only makes it worse. We discuss these and many other issues regarding CAPTCHA in Chapter 5.

Image dimensions

If the image's height and width are not specified in markup, a browser will need to download an image before creating the layout. When you provide explicit dimensions, a browser can begin showing content immediately, saving the allotted space for the image after it has a chance to download. For mobile devices, this avoids the need to rerender the page after all images have downloaded. Technically, this violates our principle of avoiding the use of presentational HTML, but there's a lot of upside for mobile applications and rendering time, and it doesn't hurt much to do. We'll say it again: for many mobile users, time is money.

```
<img width="200" height="100" src="sample.png" alt="..." />
```

Document-Level Metadata

The container for your application plug-in or your web document should contain some basic pieces of metadata to ensure the contents are rendered correctly and consistently.

Document type

The document type tells the browser how to render the page and how strictly to follow the rules for rendering. Depending on which doctype is specified and how or if it is missing altogether, browsers have three possible rendering modes: quirks, standard, and almost standard. Quirks mode is intended to display legacy pages created in 2001 or earlier—before all major browsers had implemented the final standards for HTML 4.01 and CSS Level 1.

On the mobile side of things, the bright line is between WAP 1.0 and WAP 2.0. WAP 1.0 was based on HTML but included several mobile-specific elements such as "card"—the main unit for individual web pages (as in a card deck—smaller, and more likely to fit on the smaller, mobile screen). WAP 2.0 (XHTML-MP) is built on XHTML Basic (but uses the application/vnd.wap.xhtml+xml MIME type). The following are some examples of document type declarations:

```
// Mobile - XHTML Basic 1.1
<!DOCTYPE html PUBLIC "-//W3C//DTD XHTML Basic 1.1//EN"
 "http://www.w3.org/TR/xhtml-basic/xhtml-basic11.dtd">

//XHTML Mobile Profile 1.1
<!DOCTYPE html PUBLIC "-//WAPFORUM//DTD XHTML Mobile 1.1//EN"
  "http://www.openmobilealliance.org/tech/DTD/xhtml-mobile11.dtd">

// HTML 4.01 - rendered in Standards or Almost Standards mode
// Note: lack of system identifier renders in quirks mode in IE Mac
// Transitional
<!DOCTYPE HTML PUBLIC "-//W3C//DTD HTML 4.01 Transitional//EN"
 "http://www.w3.org/TR/html4/loose.dtd">
// Strict
<!DOCTYPE HTML PUBLIC "-//W3C//DTD HTML 4.01//EN"
"http://www.w3.org/TR/html4/strict.dtd">

// XHTML 1.0 with system identifier and without an XML declaration -
// rendered in Standards or Almost Standards mode
// Transitional
<!DOCTYPE html PUBLIC "-//W3C//DTD XHTML 1.0 Transitional//EN"
"http://www.w3.org/TR/xhtml1/DTD/xhtml1-transitional.dtd">
// Strict
<!DOCTYPE html PUBLIC "-//W3C//DTD XHTML 1.0 Strict//EN"
"http://www.w3.org/TR/xhtml1/DTD/xhtml1-strict.dtd">
```

Note that including the system identifier (e.g., "*http://www .w3.org/TR/html4/strict.dtd*") can change the mode the browser uses. For a complete list of system identifiers, refer to "Comparison of document types" (*http://en.wikipedia.org/ wiki/Quirks_mode#Comparison_of_document_types*).

Language and character encoding

Declaring the language of a document ensures that Braille and synthesized speech will be generated correctly. Declaring the character encoding ensures that the correct characters are displayed in the browser or in captions in a media player. You need to specify language *and* character encoding because they indicate different things. German could be the declared language of a website, but pages can be served in a variety of character encodings, including Unicode or ISO-8859-1.

Specifying the language is straightforward—for HTML 4.01, use the `lang` attribute on the `html` element, with the ISO language code ("en" for English, "fr" for French, "es" for Spanish, "ja" for Japanese, "de" for German, and so on) as the value:

```
<!DOCTYPE HTML PUBLIC "-//W3C//DTD HTML 4.01//EN"
"http://www.w3.org/TR/html4/strict.dtd">
<html lang="de">
```

For XHTML served as XML, use the `xml:lang` attribute:

```
<!DOCTYPE html PUBLIC "-//W3C//DTD XHTML 1.1//EN"
    "http://www.w3.org/TR/xhtml11/DTD/xhtml11.dtd">
<html xmlns="http://www.w3.org/1999/xhtml" xml:lang="de">
```

For XHTML served as text/HTML, use both the `lang` and `xml:lang` attributes:

```
<!DOCTYPE html PUBLIC "-//W3C//DTD XHTML 1.0 Transitional//EN"
    "http://www.w3.org/TR/xhtml1/DTD/xhtml1-transitional.dtd">
<html xmlns="http://www.w3.org/1999/xhtml" lang="de" xml:lang="de">
```

Character encoding also depends on which MIME type your server uses and which document type you are using. The W3C Internationalization Activity's Tutorial, "Character sets & encodings in XHTML, HTML and CSS" summarizes the requirements as shown in Table 3-1.

Table 3-1. Matrix of alternatives for declaring a character encoding[a]

	HTTP headers	<?xml...	<meta...
HTML	OK	Invalid	Preferred
XHTML (text/HTML)	OK	OK	Preferred
XHTML (XML)	OK	Preferred	Invalid

[a] This table was taken from *http://www.w3.org/International/tutorials/tutorial-char-enc/#Slide0250*.

The preferred encoding is Unicode (more precisely the Universal Character Set that is defined both by ISO/IEC and Unicode standards, more simply referred to as Unicode). From the I18N tutorial:

> A Unicode encoding can support many languages and can accommodate pages and forms in any mixture of those languages. Its use also eliminates the need for server-side logic to individually determine the character encoding for each page served or each incoming form submission. This significantly reduces the complexity of dealing with a multilingual site or application.

With Unicode, there are three encoding formats to choose from: UTF-8, UTF-16, and UTF-32, depending on how many bytes are used to represent each character (1, 2, and 4, respectively). UTF-8 is most typically used. Therefore, for XHTML served as XML, here's the preferred declaration:

```
<?xml version="1.0" encoding="UTF-8" ?>
<!DOCTYPE html PUBLIC "-//W3C//DTD XHTML 1.1//EN"
    "http://www.w3.org/TR/xhtml11/DTD/xhtml11.dtd">
```

For XHTML served as text/HTML, use:

```
<!DOCTYPE html PUBLIC "-//W3C//DTD XHTML 1.0 Transitional//EN"
    "http://www.w3.org/TR/xhtml1/DTD/xhtml1-transitional.dtd">
<head>
<meta http-equiv="Content-Type" content="text/html; charset=utf-8"/>
```

Titles

Use the HTML `title` element to provide a unique title for each page/application. Titles provide landmarks for people and search engines. People use titles when switching between windows on the desktop (at this moment, I have eight tabs open in my browser). Search engine bots use titles when scanning sites. Mobile device users will use titles when downloading a page to help determine if it is in fact the page they want, and they may stop a download if a title does not match their expectations. Mobile devices may truncate the title, so frontloading the title will ensure that the most meaningful bits are more likely to show up. As the dotMobi guidelines point out, authors commonly use the site name for all pages on the site—not very useful. Put that bit at the end like so:

```
<title>Unique page title | Site Name</title>
```

Role and State

We've devoted three chapters to making web applications accessible. The primary issues with applications are:

- Making them keyboard-accessible
- Ensuring that changes caused by user interaction can be detected by a person or his software agent (whether it's a browser alone or in combination with an assistive technology)

The changes that need to be identified are primarily role and state. Knowing the role that something plays tells you about its capabilities. If it is a checkbox, you know you can check and uncheck it. If it is a button, you should be able to press it and cause something to happen. State, on the other hand, refers to how an object has changed. In the previous examples, the checkbox's states are "checked" and "unchecked." The button is "pressed" or "not pressed" or "active" or "disabled." More on that later.

Another aspect is identifying errors, which is covered in Chapter 5.

Relationships

Information about relationships is implied in the document or application structure. Using semantic elements in a good order tells a story. For example, links in an unordered list create several groups of links. These groups have relationships/data.

Why is this important? Consider the visual interface. Related objects are placed near each other. If you are unsure of one object, you often look around it to gain a better understanding of what it does. For example, a lone text field doesn't mean much until paired with its label. A single data cell in a table doesn't mean much until you compare it with other cells. The relationships between objects create the overall narrative.

We have devoted a whole chapter to how to choose the appropriate elements and attributes to create meaningful structure, but we want to foreshadow the importance of structure here by pointing out that the elements themselves have semantics and the meaning attached to those elements is metadata.

Link Text

Link by link we build paths of understanding across the web of humanity.

—Tim Berners-Lee

The link is what makes the Web—allowing us to hop, skip, and jump from information bit to information bit. The text of a link helps us predict where it goes and if we want to go there. User experience guru Jared Spool refers to link "scent" to describe users' confidence that they are getting closer to the information they seek. The more "scent" a link gives off—leading us to what we are hunting for—the less "click disappointment" we are likely to face.

For people using mobile devices, waiting for unwanted content to download is not only frustrating but also costly. A page full of "click here" links is not going to help the way a search engine ranks your site. (Want proof? Search for "click here" and see what you get.) For people using a screen reader, the links on your page may be the only pieces of information they interact with: many people pull up a list of the links on a page to get a sense of what the page is about and where they can go. In fact, most of the people visiting your site will be affected by the order and placement of links—these create context and convey meaning associated with that link.

In some cases, the design of your site or application may prevent you from making link text descriptive. In that case, the traditional advice has been to add context using the `title` attribute. Unfortunately, this is of little use to people who need that information most: screen readers need to be configured to read title text, and frequently they aren't.

A better solution is to make sense of the link with text in a span element. Then, using CSS, you can hide that extra information offscreen. This can be particularly useful when you have a number of "Click here" types of links, which can't be differentiated by screen readers as they sort through links, but you don't have free space to expand those links.

```
<a href="#">Read more<span class="context">
about providing context</span></a>
```

This CSS will hide the extra text far off the left side of the screen:

```
.context
{
   left: -999em;
   width: 1em;
   overflow: hidden;
}
```

This can be an ideal way to provide links to content in multiple formats:

```
<ul>
<li><a href="release.html"><span class="context">Press release in
 </span>HTML</a></li>
<li><a href="release.pdf"><span class="context">Press release in
</span>PDF</a></li>
<li><a href="release.doc"><span class="context">Press release in
</span>Word</a></li>
</ul>
```

Summary

Metadata helps us and our bots navigate content—whether it's a search heap or a document on our desktop. Where and to whom we navigate support our connecting with new ideas and people.

CHAPTER 4

Structure and Design

> *It is the pervading law of all things organic and inorganic,*
> *Of all things physical and metaphysical,*
> *Of all things human and all things super-human,*
> *Of all true manifestations of the head,*
> *Of the heart, of the soul,*
> *That the life is recognizable in its expression,*
> *That form ever follows function. This is the law.*
>
> —Louis Sullivan

Of all the advice we have to offer in this book, this chapter is most central to successful universal design. In fact, it is possible to follow the rest of this book and still encounter real trouble reaching more users.

Although we show examples of design using CSS, we are not visual designers by trade, and this is not a CSS design patterns book. There are many books that cover how to use CSS to style semantic code. *The Zen of CSS Design* (Peachpit Press) by Dave Shea and Molly Holzschlag is one great example. We hope to complement the creative guidance books such as theirs offer by giving you the tools to discover and overcome the universal design problems you may encounter in modern web design.

First Principles

Universal design depends not on a pixel-perfect representation of a given document or application across all screens, devices, and user scenarios, but on a structure that can be interpreted and rendered on all web-enabled devices in a manner that is faithful to the original. This means different things for different languages, as we discuss later in the book, but for HTML, it means using the document-based origins of the language to turn it into an application framework. To do that requires a strong understanding of both HTML and HTTP, and the meaning that each element and transaction carries.

GET and POST

HTTP has two primary methods of communicating with the server: GET and POST. There are other methods, but GET and POST are all that most web developers will ever need to fully understand.

A GET is a simple request containing the Uniform Resource Identifier (URI) of a specified document (in the case of the home page of a given site, the browser issues a GET request for "/"). Any other variables in this transaction are in name-value pairs as a query string, after a question mark in the URI:

```
http://www.example.com/index.php?page=news&articlename=atom
```

GETs make up more than 99% of all web requests. The default behavior of an HTML link results in a GET request being sent to the server. The rest (at least as far as those HTTP 1.0 requests issued by humans) are POSTs.

In a POST request, there are still name/value pairs sent to the server, but they are communicated differently, and with good reason. A GET request doesn't change the world around it. For example, loading up Porsche's site 1,000 times won't send 1,000 Cayennes to your door. (If you're looking to impress your colleagues, you can refer to this phenomenon as *idempotence*—in this context, it means multiple iterations of the same action have the same effect as only one.) A POST, on the other hand, *can* change the world. So, when you are registering, logging in, checking out, or doing some kind of action that cannot be undone or requires some kind of privacy or protection against happening multiple times, *you must use POST*.

One pattern that you should be aware of and know when to use is POST/Redirect/GET, sometimes called PRG. Nearly all blogs, for example, use PRG. The reason is so that when you change the world (in this case, by leaving a comment), that information is sent as a POST, and as a response—instead of showing you a confirmation page—the server redirects you to a GET request to send you back to the page you just posted to. This comes with a URI in your address bar that you can then copy to friends or bookmark, without mistakenly ending up in some posting routine, which will throw you an error.

Semantics

> [S]emantic HTML frees authors from the need to concern themselves with presentation details.*
>
> —Wikipedia, "Semantic HTML" (retrieved September 9, 2008)

* *http://en.wikipedia.org/wiki/Semantic_HTML#Semantic_HTML*

At its core, HTML is a very capable semantic language. It was designed with a wide range of expressiveness at its command. But it's only good if you, the author, use it to express what you *mean* rather than to create a visual presentation.

Please repeat after us, "Separate structure and presentation." To do this, the first step is ensuring you mark up your content with meaningful HTML. There are two HTML 4.01 elements that we will use sparingly in our examples: `div` and `span`. Along with the `class` and `id` attributes, these two elements, according to the HTML 4.01 spec, "offer a generic mechanism for adding structure to documents." That makes `div`, `span`, `id`, and `class` critical to styling with CSS. However, they don't communicate any semantics of their own. Avoid using `div` or `span` in place of an element that communicates the correct message: `blockquote` for quotes, `p` for paragraphs, `ul` and `li` for bulleted lists, and so on.

In addition, there's one element, `font`, which you will not see anywhere in our examples. The `font` element is a semantics antipattern. Used frequently to set the size, face, or color of the text, `font` leaves a hole where semantics often should be. There is no reason to use the `font` element on the Web. Ever. Even in some of the most restrictive design environments around, one of which we discuss later in the chapter.

Most of the time we see `font` still in use, it's as a replacement for a heading element. That's tragic in a number of ways:

- Using `font` is semantically no different from using `div` or `span`—which is to say, it's nonsemantic. So, where there could have been some clear structure to the document, in a place it is clearly warranted, there remains none.

- Many browsers and screen readers allow users to navigate long documents using headings, but font blocks are not headings, so those users have no heading structure to rely on.

- Worse still is the damage those sites are doing to themselves. Search engines are starving for semantics. And in a world with such poor markup practices, they are often reduced to some serious analysis simply to divine the structure of a given document. But when the engine can be certain that something is a heading, that carries weight, and as long as you don't abuse them by overloading or stuffing them, using headings along with the other structures available to you in HTML is always the best search engine strategy.

After your semantic HTML is in place, you're ready for style.

> A semantic HTML document can be paired with any number of stylesheets to provide output to computer screens (through Web browsers), high-resolution printers, handheld devices, aural browsers or braille devices for those with visual impairments, and so on. To accomplish this, nothing needs to be changed in a well-coded semantic HTML document. Readily available stylesheets make this a simple matter of pairing a semantic HTML document with the appropriate stylesheets.
>
> —Wikipedia, "Semantic HTML" (retrieved September 9, 2008)

We touch on style later in this chapter and on behaviors in Chapters 8 and 9.

Headings

We just discussed one issue that we run into often: the use of the font element to create the appearance of a heading. The greater issue is that almost any element can be styled to look like a heading. Another concern arises when images of text are used to display specific fonts.

We mentioned in the previous section that some tools allow people to navigate by headings. This may seem odd to you, but consider how someone who can see skims or scans a page. If you can see, your eye is naturally drawn to items that stand out because of differences in color, size, shape, and movement. Someone who cannot see well or at all cannot employ that same strategy to discern important items. Using semantic markup—separating presentation from structure—a tool can then make some of those judgments for the user and provide stepwise paths through the content.

Have you ever looked at an outline of a page from your site? Consider Figure 4-1. On the left is the W3C home page as it appears in most browsers. Note the different sections. How do you know they are sections? Because the use of color and borders makes them stand out. On the right is an outline of the W3C home page generated using the Firefox Web Developer Toolbar's "View document outline." This may not be exactly the same order in which a seeing eye would move through the page, but it does allow someone to discern the major sections such that they don't need to read the page top-to-bottom.

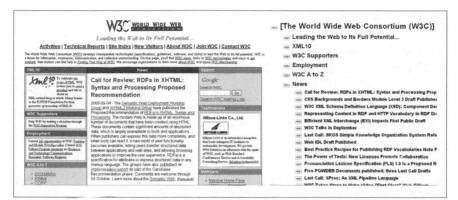

Figure 4-1. W3C home page and its outline

Links

This is a link:

```
<a href="/about">About this site</a>
```

This is not:

```
<span onclick="javascript:location.href='/about';">About this site</span>
```

Universal design dictates that you must use the tools that you have available to you in a consistent manner. JavaScript-based pseudolinking breaks both mobile and accessible usage scenarios, and confuses users with an inconsistent user interface.

In previous sections, we discussed semantic markup and the need to separate presentation from structure. In this case, we need to separate semantics from behavior. In Chapter 8, you'll learn about Unobtrusive JavaScript—how to use JavaScript as an enhancement rather than out of necessity. With the second example, a browser, screen reader, or search engine will not identify this as a link—therefore you lose all of the benefits of the semantic markup.

In Chapter 9, we will teach you about WAI-ARIA—a specification to make Ajax accessible through additional HTML markup. Even if the earlier example were identified using the ARIA role of "link," the ARIA Best Practices guide recommends, "Use the native markup as well as possible."

You may have a really great reason to use this markup, but before you do, please read about Unobtrusive JavaScript (Chapter 8) and ARIA (Chapter 9).

Tables

A lot of misconceptions exist about tables, and historical problems with accessibility and mobile contexts are to blame. But then, so is David Siegal.

Siegal wrote this truly awful book called *Creating Killer Web Sites* (Hayden), which unleashed a whole wave of hacks—the single-pixel spacer GIF and layout tables being the most intractable—on the web design public. It took years before Cascading Style Sheets (CSS) arrived and began to stem the tide. (In his defense, Siegal did apologize for having "ruined the Web" in 1997.)

But then came the backlash. With the web standards movement of the early 2000s, the pendulum swung toward madness in the opposite direction. Web standards advocates pushed back against using tables for layout so strenuously that many began to believe that tables themselves were bad. We have had people tell us that their site policy is to not use tables. At all. Even for tabular data!

So, let's reset. Tables for data are good. (Really, really good.) That's what tables are designed to do: relay data. The best way to mark up multivariate data, from census results to phone lists to sports scores, is with a table. Got it? Great. Tell your crazy friend who's still doing it all with divs to read Chapter 6.

On the other hand, tables for layout aren't so good.

If you must keep using your layout tables, make sure that they're streamlined as much as possible and that the visual order they indicate is the same as the way they're read in a screen reader. That is the real problem being masked by layout table hysteria. If that's not a problem for you, and you like how your site renders on mobile devices, take your time extricating yourself from the situation, and focus on higher-priority fixes. Ultimately, though, in the interest of making the experience better for all of your users, you should do what is necessary to wean yourself off of layout tables.

Lists

Lists provide a variety of semantic information, primarily groupings. One of the most common uses of lists these days is for creating menus. The basic structure is a list (CSS is used to hide submenu items and position the menu bar horizontally or vertically), and then the behavior is layered on top of that (through CSS and/or JavaScript).

There are three ways to make a list, and the differences among them provide additional information about the list items and the relationships between them:

The unordered list (UL)
  Used for bulleted lists

The ordered list (OL)
  Used for numbered lists

The definition list (DL)
  Used for associations between two related pieces of data

Why use a list instead of paragraphs with icons that make it look like a list? As with headers, when people see a list they start to process it as a chunk of information that they can either skip or delve into. An ordered list helps users discern the priority or ordering implied in the list. When looking at a definition list, it's clear which items are terms and which are definitions. Providing the semantics allows tools to communicate this information to people. Tommy Olsson has a good article about lists that may help you understand what we are talking about: "When Is a List Not a List?" (*http://www.autisticcuckoo.net/ archive.php?id=2007/08/07/lists*).

Color

The use of color in your web application can have a positive or negative impact on your users, depending on their ability to discern your color choices. Most issues relate to color differentiation and color contrast, and they can affect mobile users as well as those with vision-related disabilities.

Color Differentiation

The ability to see color accurately is occasionally a barrier to people with one of a number of forms of colorblindness. For example, one of the most common color combinations in user interfaces for Western users is red for stop/no/ cancel and green for go/yes/OK—yet this same combination correlates strongly with protanopia, or red-green colorblindness, a condition that affects up to 4% of men of European descent. Color can also make things difficult for users whose mobile browsers are rerendering images as text or don't have color displays.

These problems are easy to solve, without necessarily changing your color scheme. All you need to do is associate a textual label to anything that communicates its meaning purely by color. It's sufficient to have, for example, "OK" in your green button (with alt text to match, naturally), in which case, you could refer to the button like so: "Click on the green OK button to proceed." This avoids referring to the button color alone as in "Click on the green button to proceed."

A growing number of tools simulate color deficiencies. See the section "Question 6: Nonsensory operation" in Chapter 11 for more information about them.

Color Contrast

Subtle contrasts between text and background are frequently a source of trouble for users. It may be tempting to put light blue text onto a medium blue background, or light gray on white, but that could make it difficult or impossible to read that text, especially on handheld devices. High contrast between foreground and background will make it that much easier for everyone.

There are tools available to test color contrast values. Again, see the section "Question 6. Nonsensory operation" in Chapter 11 for more about them.

CSS Highlights

Assuming that you've marked up the structure of your document with many well-meaning elements, we'll now turn to CSS to transform your well-organized outline into a multicolumned, colorful beauty. However, this is just the tip of the iceberg; of course, we focus on issues related to universal design. If you are new to CSS, check out a comprehensive CSS reference (anything by Eric Meyer or Christopher Schmitt).

Liquid Layout

One of the first concepts to introduce is units of measure, as they are a key component in designing a *liquid layout*. Early web designers were making the transition from print design to the Web. In print, you have fixed layouts that are precisely defined and static—they are "pixel-perfect." But those designers had no control over which browser someone used, or the size of the browser window, or the size of the text, which meant that their pixel-perfect designs weren't very perfect.

As HTML and CSS evolved, designers realized they could create designs that would reflow to accommodate browser version, window size, and text characteristics. Instead of seeing everything as absolutely positioned, designers started thinking in terms of relative positions.

Thus, there are three ways to specify length: relative units, absolute units, and percentages. Here are the definitions from the CSS2.1 specification:[†]

[†] *http://www.w3.org/TR/CSS21/*

Relative length units specify a length relative to another length property. Style sheets that use relative units will more easily scale from one medium to another (e.g., from a computer display to a laser printer).

Relative units are:

- em: the 'font-size' of the relevant font
- ex: the 'x-height' of the relevant font
- px: pixels, relative to the viewing device

Absolute length units are only useful when the physical properties of the output medium are known.

The absolute units are:

- in: inches—1 inch is equal to 2.54 centimeters.
- cm: centimeters
- mm: millimeters
- pt: points—the points used by CSS 2.1 are equal to 1/72nd of an inch.
- pc: picas —1 pica is equal to 12 points.

Percentage values are always relative to another value[.]

—CSS 2.1 Specification, W3C Recommendation

The most commonly used units are em, px, and percentages, and they are all relative to something else (whether it be another length property or another element) and reflow differently.

Text Size

In terms of accessibility to users with disabilities, text size has become somewhat less of a problem recently. Firefox 3 and Internet Explorer 7 each adopted full-page zoom, a feature that's been in the Opera browser for years. This kind of zooming increases the size of every element on the page—text, images, tables, even Flash objects—in contrast to the old model, on which only the text itself is magnified. MobileSafari uses this feature most often; it's how users pinch and expand documents on the iPhone.

Of course, this shift isn't necessarily always an improvement. For example, if you're a user who wants text to be twice as large, full-page zoom also doubles the column width, and depending on the kind of display, that could require users to scroll left to right, line by line through long passages of text. Thus, it is still important to set your font sizes using relative units so that users can override them without having to resort to zooming.

Positioning

If you have used semantic HTML, there's not much that using CSS will do to break it. We won't say much about positioning here, but we do have a lot to say about it and its effects in Chapter 8.

Images

A great use of CSS's ability to include images is background images: they are decorative and don't need a text equivalent. However, using background images for images that convey important information is not a good idea unless that information is available in the text of the page. General rule: if it's *purely* decorative, it's cool to use CSS to include it; if the image conveys important information, use the `img` element with an `alt` attribute (see Chapter 3 for information about using the `alt` attribute).

Text Versus Images of Text

Web content is reaching a turning point with respect to the treatment of text. In fact, there are two major changes that will have a near-term impact on text on the Web: full-page zoom and web fonts. During this transition, though, there will still be millions of users who aren't up on the new tech, so it's important to look at what works now, and determine for yourself how to write your content so that you can transition without stress.

What works now

In the Firefox 2/IE 6 era, the zoom function of the browser caused the fonts to resize but not the remainder of the document's structure. The result was text that was often smashed together or short lines of chunky text in increasingly absurd layouts. To address this, it was recommended to design documents using CSS rather than tables and to use relative CSS units so that the document would resize along with (or around) the larger fonts. On the other hand, full-page zoom increases the entire page's dimensions, including images, tables—you name it. *While we still emphasize using CSS for layout*, it's not strictly necessary for full-page zoom. CSS-based layouts will, however, come in handy when your page is transformed in mobile browsers.

Web fonts are another story. Due to a couple of unproductive attempts at web fontography, the Web has been limited to a small subset of the fonts currently available in TrueType, OpenType, or Adobe Type 1 format, to wit:

- Times New Roman
- Helvetica (or Arial)

- Courier (or Courier New)
- Verdana
- Tahoma
- Georgia
- Trebuchet MS
- Impact

In other words, this is the limited set of fonts that are common to both Windows and Mac operating systems. However, many *nix (Unix and Linux) machines do not have these fonts.

A lot of people haven't been very happy with this, and there have been many, many different attempts at trying to bridge that gap. Most of these were image replacement schemes that used CSS tricks to replace semantic HTML headings with images, ostensibly offering the best of both worlds. One of the first to take hold was Fahrner Image Replacement (FIR). The idea, named after creator Todd Fahrner, hid the heading text and replaced it with an image with the bitmapped text. Unfortunately, what was good for semanticists was not necessarily good for universal design. Namely, using FIR, screen readers no longer read the heading text at all.

Various other alternatives popped up, with various positive and negative effects. With image replacement, one big downside is that the images all have to be preauthored and sized to the area they're supposed to fill, making the approach fragile and time-consuming. With that in mind, Mike Davidson adapted a technique created by Shaun Inman, and Scalable Inman Flash Replacement (sIFR) was born.

What About Search Engines?

You may wonder if image replacement may hurt your ranking with search engines, but our latest information indicates there's nothing to fear. Our friend and colleague Dave Shea asked about it in May 2008, and the conclusion he was led to was that as long as you're not trying to fool search engines (say, with an image that said "Welcome to my site!" replacing "Free Miley Cyrus/ Hannah Montana MP3s!"), then Google et al. won't penalize you.

The principal advantage of sIFR over image replacement schemes is that any heading can be rendered in nearly any antialiased font you like. It takes some configuring, with a separate style sheet and a JavaScript file you have to customize and embed, but once that's done, you can set, for example, every H4 to appear in red Trajan Pro. Better, if your users don't have Flash (such as, say, iPhone users), the heading itself degrades gracefully.

Alas, sIFR has its limitations as well. Like image replacement, when you select a span of text that includes a sIFR heading, the heading text won't be included. You'll need a copy of Flash and the font you want. And you don't want to use it for more than a couple headers per page, or you risk dramatically increasing the load time. That said, it works with screen readers, it's pretty, it's reasonably simple, and it's much more fun than sitting in Photoshop, churning out GIFs.

But still, when there's a better way, use it.

For examples, documentation, and a support forum for the sIFR technique, read Mike Davidson's blog "sIFR 2.0: Rich Accessible Typography for the Masses" at *http://www.mikeindustries.com/blog/sifr/*.

Web fonts

One approach to the limited number of fonts on the Web has been floating around almost as long as the Web itself. As early as 1997—the golden age of the browser wars—embedded or downloadable fonts saw implementations in Internet Explorer 4 and Netscape 4. Naturally, as with much of the ingenuity of that era, they were incompatible with each other: Microsoft based its embedded fonts on OpenType, while Netscape partnered with Bitstream. For a long time, nothing happened, and eventually the wind was gone from the web fonts' sails.

Today, thanks at least in part to a new CSS-support arms race, a new round of web font mania has arrived. Opera Software has announced support for the web fonts module of CSS3, published as a working draft in 2002 by the W3C. The developers of WebKit, from which Safari and Konqueror are drawn, have also announced they're working on web fonts, and Microsoft is rumored to be in the mix as well with Internet Explorer 8.

You may think that web fonts will finally make your life easier. But they won't. Especially when you're thinking about increasing your audience. Most mobile devices won't ever bother to process embedded fonts in CSS. It's simply too much to ask of devices with limited bandwidth and processing power. Using arbitrary fonts has implications for readability as well, given that not all fonts are created equal, and many designers, to put it lightly, are not known for their restraint.

An even bigger problem, though, is internationalization. If your style sheet is ever going to be used with content in several languages, you will need to ensure that the fonts you select contain glyphs in all of those scripts (Japanese, simplified and traditional Chinese, Hebrew, Arabic, Indic scripts, and so on). One advantage of local fonts is that these issues have long ago been sorted out. Issuing just-in-time font selections will certainly expose the poor support in many otherwise very pretty fonts for scripts other than Latin.

Flicker and Patterns

In 1997, an episode of *Pokemon* airing in Japan made the world take note of the phenomenon of photoepilepsy. Some 685 Japanese children and adults were taken by ambulance to hospitals, suffering from seizures, convulsions, blurred vision, headaches, dizziness, and nausea, after watching a scene of the cartoon in which much of the screen flashed blue and red at a rate of 12 hertz (12 times per second).

The same potential to cause seizures exists in web content as well, and WCAG 1.0 restricts flashing content, instructing authors to avoid anything that flashes between 4 and 59 Hz. Section 508 also bans flashing content in the range of 2–55 Hz.

In the aftermath of the *Pokemon* incident, however, much research has been done to determine what colors, at what saturation levels, at what flashing frequencies, and in what percentage of the viewable field can trigger these seizures. With this information in hand, WCAG 2.0 now specifies more granular advice. Here's what it says:

> Web pages do not contain anything that flashes more than three times in any one-second period...

OK, that's the rule of thumb. If you need to dig deeper than that, prepare for some hard science. Here are the qualifiers if you want content that flashes faster than 3 Hz:

- A flash or rapidly changing image sequence is below the threshold (i.e., content passes) if any of the following are true:
  - There are no more than three General Flashes and/or no more than three Red Flashes within any one-second period; or
  - The combined area of flashes occurring concurrently occupies no more than a total of .006 steradians within any 10-degree visual field on the screen (25% of any 10-degree visual field on the screen) at typical viewing distance

where:

- A General Flash is defined as a pair of opposing changes in relative luminance of 10% or more of the maximum relative luminance where the relative luminance of the darker image is below 0.80; and where "a pair of opposing changes" is an increase followed by a decrease, or a decrease followed by an increase; and
- A Red Flash is defined as any pair of opposing transitions involving a saturated red.

> *Exception:* flashing that is a fine, balanced pattern such as white noise or an alternating checkerboard pattern with "squares" smaller than 0.1 degree (of visual field at typical viewing distance) on a side does not violate the thresholds.

There. Got that?

That "10-degree visual field" is the important part. As the WCAG 2.0 Guidelines explain, that amounts to a 341x256 rectangle on a 15" to 17" 1024x768 display, viewed from 22"–26" away. If it's smaller than that, you're good to go. For anything larger, you may need to limit the flash rate. Tools to analyze your content's conformance to this requirement are available and will likely become easier to find as support for WCAG 2.0 increases.

Designing for Email

We talk about using almost exclusively modern techniques to achieve universal design. Still, there's one area where the most universal approach is somewhat less elegant: HTML email.

The main problem with email clients is that their support for HTML is extremely inconsistent. In some cases, such as with Gmail and Hotmail, many CSS styles are sandboxed to prevent changes from affecting the rest of their web-based interfaces. In other cases, such as with Outlook 2007, the client's HTML parser doesn't support the CSS box model (that is, the padding, border, and margin properties), so high-fidelity layout doesn't stand a chance.

In fact, support for HTML email is so unreliable that a group called the Email Standards Project, modeled after the Web Standards Project (WaSP), has been formed to guide email client vendors in the right direction. If WaSP's work with browser vendors is any indicator, though, it will be several years before there is a common email platform. With that in mind, here are some tips for designing HTML-based emails:

- Use layout tables. Just don't go overboard with them. Fragile things that they are, email client HTML parsers aren't going to reliably handle deeply nested tables, so keep it down to a single, basic table.

- Keep formatting to a minimum. Realize that pixel-perfect rendering is a pipe dream in the medium of email, and design accordingly. Don't send lots of images that have to be aligned just so, or you will be disappointed with the results.

- Use CSS for font selection. All but the most ill-suited clients support CSS on fonts, even where they fail elsewhere.

- Send a plain-text version. One of the few advantages of email over the Web model is that you can send multiple data types simultaneously, and you should have a text-only version of the content you wish to send. That will suit users of mobile devices just fine, and those who prefer HTML will never be presented with that text.
- If possible, include links so that people can view the email as a web page, which will render better in a browser than in an email client.

Summary

Structure plays a critical role in universal design because it gives each user and device enough information to present your content in a way that's most logical to the user's situation. It's important to understand the semantic implications of each of the elements of your language of choice and use them as faithfully as possible.

Be aware that color is not perceived in the same way universally. Complications can arise with device capabilities, as well as issues with colorblindness or color deficiency. Keep this in mind throughout the visual design of the page so that problems don't present themselves later on, and remember, don't use color alone to indicate meaning.

CHAPTER 5

Forms

> *Be conservative in what you do; be liberal in*
> *what you accept from others.*
>
> —Postel's Law, from RFC 793, the
> Transmission Control Protocol (TCP)
> specification

If the most important feature of the Web is the link, the form is a close second. It goes without saying that forms are integral to the web experience. And yet, so often such little attention is paid to how we use them. Anyone who's used the Web for any period of time has likely experienced frustrating cryptic error messages, random failures, or worst of all, lost data.

While researching for this book, Matt encountered a survey site that inexplicably *didn't* use HTML checkbox or radio button controls to collect results from users. In their place were images that changed when clicked and didn't completely behave like HTML controls, making it extremely frustrating to work through. Imagine a company asking you to fill out a 50-question survey (a big enough inconvenience on its own) and finding that you couldn't tab from field to field and hit the space bar to check or uncheck items. Worse still, imagine you get to the bottom of the page, click on the image reading "Submit", and nothing happens. Now imagine your impression of the company that put you through all that, as you retrieve the laptop you just threw across the room.

These days, the stakes are higher than ever. E-commerce sites need simple checkout procedures that make their customers feel satisfied with their experience—and confident enough to make purchases. Other services such as webmail, collaboration tools, or financial sites need to protect user data, minimize errors, and recover gracefully at all times. If not, there's invariably somewhere else users can go. It's no longer acceptable to require a certain browser or version, to reject mobile device users, or to force users through complicated workflows.

Forms are the enablers of two-way interaction between sites and users, fostering both community and commerce. And that means it's critical to build them well.

In this chapter, we show how to use HTML form controls in a way that will prepare you not only for mobile and assistive technology (AT) users, but for Ajax users as well. We cover how to use CSS to get the visual layout you need, how to use scripts to handle validation on the client side, and how to set up a keyboard navigation order.

Labels

HTML has plenty of underused elements, but perhaps the most useful of them is `label`. It's easy to see who has taken universal design into account in their forms: just click on the labels in one of their forms. If the focus moves to the form field as a result, they're using labels. For people who are familiar with the user interface practices in Windows, this is especially handy; for users of assistive technology, it's more of a necessity because there is no other way to explicitly associate labels with the form fields they represent. But very few authors either know that they can extend those practices to the Web or take the few seconds necessary to do it.

Let's start with the basic username and password field:

```
<form method="post"  action="/login" >
<label for="username">Username:</label><br/>
<input type="text"  name="username"  id="username" size=" 10"
maxlength="10"/><br/>
<label for="password">Password:</label><br/>
<input type="password"  name="password" id="password" size=" 10"
 maxlength="10">
</form>
```

 Note the use of the `label` element and the `for` attribute. The `label` element is more semantic than `b` or **strong** or anything else, and the `for` attribute allows you to explicitly associate the two. Associate `for` with the `id` of the field in question, not the `name`.

fieldset and legend

Another underutilized HTML feature is `fieldset`, which is designed to group form controls together. With `fieldset` and its complementary `legend` element, you can wrap these fields both visually and in a structure that improves their appearance on both mobile devices and screen readers.

For example, say you want to organize billing addresses and shipping addresses separately. Here's the actual code, using similar CSS as that we'll discuss in the upcoming "Tab Order" section:

```
<fieldset>
  <legend>Billing Address</legend>
  <div id="column1">
    <label for="billstreet">Street</label> <br/>
    <label for="billcity">City</label> <br/>
    <label for="billprovince">Province</label> <br/>
    <label for="billpostalcode">Postal Code</label>
  </div>
  <div id="column2">
    <input type="text" name="billstreet" id="billstreet"><br/>
    <input type="text" name="billcity" id="billcity"/><br/>
    <input type="text" name="billprovince" id="billprovince"><br/>
    <input type="text" name="billpostalcode" id="billpostalcode">
  </div>
</fieldset>
```

Figure 5-1 shows what that code looks in Firefox.

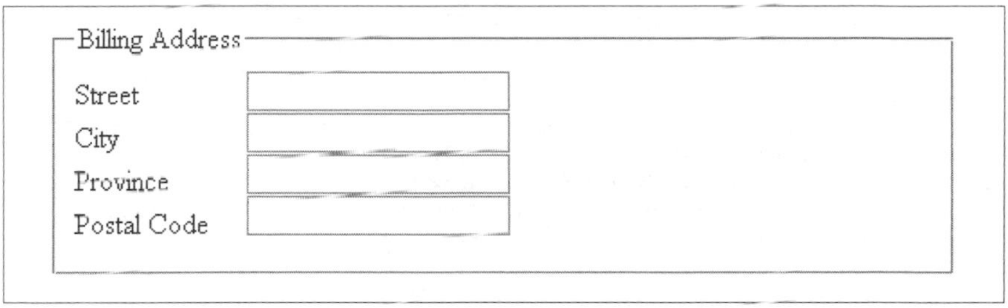

Figure 5-1. Screenshot of fieldset and legend elements example

Screen readers use this information as well. JAWS, for example, will read the legend before each field contained in the fieldset ("billing address street, billing address city, billing address province..."), providing users with enough information to know which address they're editing at any given moment.

What About the iPhone?

The iUI library (*http://code.google.com/p/iui/*) is a combination of JavaScript and CSS that renders semantic HTML in the iPhone's native user experience. When you use semantic code such as `label` and `fieldset`, an iPhone user will see what is shown in Figure 5-2.

See how the labels are inside the text fields? That's done with iPhone-specific CSS. With this library or others like it, you can optimize larger forms for the iPhone, without your desktop browser users noticing. Isn't universal design great?

Just add some classes to your existing HTML:

```html
<body>
    <div class="toolbar">
        <h1 id="pageTitle"></h1>
        <a id="backButton" class="button" href="#"></a>
    </div>

    <ul id="home" title="Order info" selected="true">

        <li class="group">Address</li>
        <li><a href="#billing">Billing Address</a></li>
        <li><a href="#shipping">Shipping Address</a></li>

        <li class="group">Payment info</li>
        <li><a href="#credit">Credit card</a></li>
    </ul>


<form id="billing" class="dialog" action="/order" method="POST">
        <fieldset>
        <legend>Billing Address</legend>
    <label for="billstreet">Street</label> <input type="text"
 name="billstreet" id="billstreet">
        <label for="billcity">City</label> <input type="text" name="billcity"
id="billcity">
        <label for="billprovince">Province</label> <input type="text"
name="billprovince" id="billprovince">
        <label for="billpostalcode">Postal Code</label> <input type="text"
name="billpostalcode" id="billpostalcode">
        <a class="button leftButton" type="cancel">Cancel</a>
    <a class="button blueButton" type="submit">Save</a>
        </fieldset>
</form>

</body>
```

OK, we cheated a little. It takes a little extra code to render the legend like this, but it's not too bad. The full source for this example is available on the book's website, at *http:// ud4wa.com*.

The accesskey Attribute

You may be aware of an attribute named accesskey. It was added to HTML 4 as an accessibility feature and was intended to associate a given keystroke with a control in the document.

So why, then, aren't we recommending it? It's complicated. So complicated, in fact, that each major browser implements accesskey differently.

Figure 5-2. Using HTML, CSS, and JavaScript to create an iPhone look and feel with iUI

If that wasn't confusing enough, there are more problems. In Internet Explorer (IE), you press the Alt key and the specified key to activate the **accesskey**. But IE already uses Alt+key combinations in its interface: Alt+F for the File menu, Alt+H for Help, and so on. On top of that, those keystrokes change from language to language. So really, if you want to ensure that your accesskeys will actually help, you're ultimately limited to numbers. The British government specified a standardized list of controls, which is helpful but not broadly implemented, as is the fate of nearly every ad hoc content standard.

And further, the accesskey's capabilities are different from browser to browser. For example, an accesskey on a link in Firefox 3 and Opera 9.5 follows that link, while it only focuses on that link in IE 6 and 7. The differences are summarized in Table 5-1.

Table 5-1. Activating accesskeys—differences in browser behavior

	Shortcut key(s)	Activates or focuses controls?
Internet Explorer 6	Alt+key	Activates
Opera	Shift+Esc, key	Activates
Firefox 2	Shift+Alt+key	Focuses
Firefox 3	Shift+Alt+key	Activates
Safari 3 for Windows	Alt+key	Focuses
Safari 3 for Mac OS X	Ctrl+key	Focuses

Due to all this complexity, we recommend that you *do not rely on accesskeys.* There are standards-based approaches, such as the XHTML 1.1 Access Module, which may help resolve this problem in the future. But for the time being, if you need keyboard shortcuts, it's better to use event handlers in JavaScript, at the window level.

While people designing primarily for the desktop experience are happy to heed our advice, mobile developers have a different opinion. In the mobile realm, accesskeys are encouraged:

> You should code your links with accesskeys, so that the user can use the phone keypad to navigate links. We recommend assigning up to ten accesskeys to any page (0–9) to ensure compatibility with older devices.
>
> —dotMobi Mobile Web Developers Guide, page 15

Tab Order

While `accesskey` has its problems, there's little reason to ignore the `tabindex` attribute. Setting a useful tab order is good for all keyboard users, including those using screen readers or onscreen keyboards. Most mobile browsers ignore `tabindex` in favor of navigating with the arrow keys—which makes sense when you remember very few of them have a Tab key to begin with. Because of this, `tabindex` fits with the principles of universal design: it offers a benefit to one class of users, without side effects for others.

 Be sure to keep `tabindex` values up-to-date. When new content is added, test that the tab order still makes sense and update `tabindex` values accordingly.

The `tabindex` attribute is not called for unless the fields being tabbed to are somehow out of order. Most commonly, this happens when using a layout table to form two columns of form controls:

```
<table>
    <tr>
        <td>
            <label for="firstname">First name:</label>
            <input type="text" name="firstname" id="firstname" />
        </td>
        <td>
            <label for="cardtype">Credit Card: </label>
            <select name="cardtype" id="cardtype">
                <option>MasterCard</option>
                <option>Visa</option>
                <option>American Express</option>
            </select>
        </td>
    </tr>
    <tr>
        <td>
            <label for="lastname">Last name:</label>
            <input type="text" name="lastname" id="lastname" />
        </td>
        <td>
            <label for="cardnumber">Card Number:</label>
            <input type="text" name="cardnumber" id="cardnumber" />
        </td>
    </tr>
</table>
```

This code is for a simple table with first and last name on the left and credit card information on the right. But structurally, the name and credit card fields are interleaved, and this is how they will appear in the tab order. Users will go from first name, to credit card type, to last name, to credit card number, and so on, down the page. For anybody who uses the Tab key to move between fields, this can be disorienting.

We can work around this by setting the `tabindex` attribute on our form fields, like so:

```
<table>
    <tr>
        <td>
            <label for="firstname">First name:</label>
            <input type="text" name="firstname" id="firstname"
                tabindex="10" />
        </td>
        <td>
            <label for="cardtype">Credit Card: </label>
            <select name="cardtype" id="cardtype" tabindex="110">
                <option>MasterCard</option>
                <option>Visa</option>
```

```
                    <option>American Express</option>
                </select>
            </td>
        </tr>
        <tr>
            <td>
                <label for="lastname">Last name:</label>
                <input type="text" name="lastname" id="lastname"
                tabindex="20" />
            </td>
            <td>
                <label for="cardnumber">Card Number:</label>
                <input type="text" name="cardnumber" id="cardnumber"
                tabindex="120" />
            </td>
        </tr>
        ...
    </table>
```

Now the tab order will flow from first name (10) to last name (20) to card type (110) to card number (120). We use multiples of 10 here because it'll be easier to add, say, a middle name or a cardholder name, in between these existing fields later on. We assume that there may be up to 10 fields on the left, so we just jumped by 100 to the right. We have plenty of space with tabindex—up to 32767—so we may as well use it.

The Four tabindexes

How tab order is handled varies by technology. For example:

- In HTML 4.01 and XHTML 1.x and 2, items that do not have a tabindex value appear in the tab order *after* items with a set value. Also, only items that normally receive tab focus (that is, form fields and links) may have a tabindex attribute.

- In HTML 5, *any* visible element may have a tabindex attribute, and you can exclude certain items from the tab order by setting tabindex to –1 (although it can still be programmatically focused, as we'll see in Chapter 8).

- In Flash 7 and lower, any object can have a tabindex property, but once you set it for one object, you must set it for *all* of them, or tabbing will follow the player default sequence rather than the assigned order.

- In Flash 8 and higher, you may set tabindex for any object, but those objects without it will not appear in the tab order.

There is, however, a better way. Since mobile users don't have wide displays, they're not going to want to scroll sideways to move from field to field. In general, it's better in cases like this to structure our form the way we want it using the language's built-in features, and style it separately.

In the case of our form shown earlier, we can do something like this instead:

```
<div id="column1">
    <label for="firstname">First name:</label>
    <input type="text" name="firstname" id="firstname" />
    <label for="lastname">Last name:</label>
    <input type="text" name="lastname" id="lastname"/>
</div>
<div id="column2">
    <label for="cardtype">Credit Card: </label>
    <select name="cardtype" id="cardtype">
        <option>MasterCard</option>
        <option>Visa</option>
        <option>American Express</option>
    </select>
    <label for="cardnumber">Card Number:</label>
    <input type="text" name="cardnumber" id="cardnumber" />
</div>
```

Then we can use CSS to lay them side by side:

```
#column1, #column2 {
    width: 49%;
    border: 0;
    margin: 0 auto;
    padding: 3px 0;
}
#column1 {
    float:left;
}
#column2 {
    float:right;
}
```

Now, most mobile devices will just ignore your CSS, or read your separate handheld style sheet. If you leave out styling on those divs, you end up with a form that displays very cleanly in a single row.

But wait. What happened to our tabindex values? We don't need them! Most of the time, if you structure your code as simply as possible, there's no need for tabindex. But it's good to know that it's always there when you really need it.

We may be able to improve our form even more by using some more semantics. Let's rebuild this form using a definition list, or dl. The dl element and its children, dt and dd, are meant to convey a relationship between two items. According to the specification, it need not be, strictly speaking, a definition.

```
<dl id="column1">
    <dt><label for="firstname">First name:</label></dt>
    <dd><input type="text" name="firstname" id="firstname" /></dd>
    <dt><label for="lastname">Last name:</label></dt>
    <dd><input type="text" name="lastname" id="lastname" /></dd>
</dl>
<dl id="column2">
    <dt><label for="cardtype">Credit Card: </label></dt>
    <dd><select name="cardtype" id="cardtype">
        <option>MasterCard</option>
        <option>Visa</option>
        <option>American Express</option>
    </select></dd>
    <dt><label for="cardnumber">Card Number:</label></dt>
    <dd><input type="text" name="cardnumber" id="cardnumber" /></dd>
</dl>
```

We gain a few more side benefits with this approach. First of all, the CSS we just wrote works the same as before. `dl`, like `div`, is a block element, so we can set margin and padding values on it. And we can gain two small victories for certain groups of users:

- For users of mobile devices that don't support CSS, the label and the form field are now associated in a manner that is relevant for their devices.

- We may prefer one number spanning both columns, but some information is better than none. Like we said, it's a small victory.

This is exemplary of the universal design aesthetic. We've used our language's built-in functionality to improve the experience for everyone, by giving each user's device enough information to render the form more appropriately. And we can make changes like this in a gradual fashion, without disorienting our users.

We run into `tabindex` again in Chapter 8.

Error Handling

Perhaps the most important feature of forms is one that's completely unspecified in HTML: validation.

It used to be that all problems were handled on the server. HTML and HTTP were just the go-between and didn't interfere with anything except, for example, the maximum length of a given text field.

Forms are funny things, and people are even funnier. The longer and more complex a form gets, the more likely that something is going to be wrong with what is submitted. It's missing a required field. A zip code field has too few

---

digits or isn't relevant (for the 95% of people who don't have mailing addresses in the U.S.). Or maybe the perfectly valid credit card is perfectly out of credit.

JavaScript has made itself invaluable when it comes to most error conditions; so much so, in fact, that we consider client-side form validation more or less mandatory. What used to be a reasonable delay—the round-trip to the server to find out the results of your form—is now a real inconvenience, especially when your problem could have been fixed immediately.

Communicating error and warning conditions to users is not a standard process—but it is something that you will need to do frequently enough that you should have a plan. Here, too, we need to make sure that the plan includes the most inclusive ways of notifying users of their errors.

Client Side

The first step you should take with your forms validation is to determine what could possibly break. Here are some of the obvious potential failures:

- A required field is blank.
- A numeric field contains letters, or vice versa.
- A checkbox (for example, indicating that you have read the Terms and Conditions) has not been checked.
- A credit card field does not contain the correct number of digits or fails mod-10 validation (a simple algorithm to check that a card number isn't an obvious fake).
- A credit card number doesn't match its type (Visa starts with 4, Master-Card with 5, etc.).

There are less obvious ones to prepare for as well:

- An expense report requires a decimal figure.
- A date, phone number, email address, or URL field needs to be formatted.
- The subject line of an email is empty.
- A value is outside of a given range (e.g., a 7 on a scale of 1 to 5).

Each of these falls into one of three categories:

Errors
   Constraint violations or other errors that require user intervention
Warnings
   Problems that may require the user's attention but could still be part of a valid submission

Formatting issues
> Problems that may require the user's attention or may be solved algorithmically

It's possible to test each field after the user is done entering data, but this can cause unwanted side effects. For example, let's say you check every field of your form each time a user hits the Tab key, and alert the user if any field is invalid—a common practice on the Web. Your validator detects that the user skipped over a field, and an error message pops up. And then another. And another. Each time the user changes fields.

Simple enough, you say. The user can just mouse back to that field and fix it. Then, what does someone who's using only a keyboard—or a keypad—have to do? She'll have to arrow or tab all the way back to the offending field—getting hit with an alert box every step of the way.

It's better to validate your form just in time. When you're about to send a message to the server is when you should inform the user of any changes he needs to make.

Required fields need to be marked somehow. In HTML 4.01, there's no semantic markup for that, so we have to wing it. Put an asterisk inside the `label` element of each form field that's required. Better yet, put the word "Required." Or, if you're short on space, you could insert an image of an asterisk, and go a little bit out of the way to inform screen-reader users of the constraint:

```
<img src="asterisk.gif" alt="Required field"/>
```

How you notify the user of errors also has an impact. JavaScript alert boxes are fine but only if there's one of them. If you have 15 errors you want a user to solve, employ that one alert box to tell her how many things she'll have to fix.

Another thing that you can do is set the focus on the form field containing the first error. Providing text that indicates what is wrong, in close proximity to and programmatically associated with the field, is a good approach. That way, people using smaller displays as well as those using screen readers don't have to scroll to the top or bottom of the screen to be reminded which field is incomplete.

What about formatting issues? Fix them yourself. Users aren't happy when they enter their phone number with dashes, only to be told they need to enter it with parentheses, or that they have to enter superfluous dashes to their credit card number. You're the one taking the money. And you know that 10 digits add up to a valid U.S. phone number and that 16 or 17 digits make up a valid credit card number. Shouldn't you be doing some of the work instead of raising the hackles of your customers?

Server Side

Keep in mind that client-side validation doesn't protect you from having to check user input on the server. If you don't, you may have problems ranging from a mismatch in constraints between the JavaScript validation and your database, to security exploits attempting to bring down or take over your server. If JavaScript is off or unavailable, users may unknowingly bring about these conditions. Always check what you receive, and prepare to generate error messages matching the ones you're creating on the client side.

Remember Postel's Law. We opened the chapter with it: "Be conservative in what you do; be liberal in what you accept from others." The late Jon Postel was a really smart guy, and the principle that bears his name has been reconstituted throughout the specifications that run the Internet. Another IETF Request for Comment, RFC 1122, expands on Postel's Law in a way that syncs nicely with the needs of server-side validation:

> Software should be written to deal with every conceivable error, no matter how unlikely; sooner or later a packet will come in with that particular combination of errors and attributes, and unless the software is prepared, chaos can ensue. [...] Adaptability to change must be designed into all levels of Internet host software.
>
> —*http://tools.ietf.org/html/rfc1122*

CAPTCHA

Nearly everyone who uses the Web has run into those annoying little pictures of text that you're supposed to read to prove that you're a human being. They're known as Completely Automated Public Turing Tests to Tell Computers and Humans Apart (CAPTCHAs). And they've been Public Enemy #1 for blind, low-vision, and dyslexic people for years.

In May 2008, Matt appeared with the creator of CAPTCHA, Luis von Ahn, on an episode of *ACB Radio*, a web radio show put on by the American Council of the Blind. What von Ahn had to offer to his audience was not a rousing defense of his creation but a thoughtful acknowledgment of what accessibility advocates have said all along: it's not a cure for cancer, and its use comes at the cost of excluding an increasing number of real people from services they should be able to access. Go here to listen to the show: *http://www.acbradio .org/archives/mainmenu/ml341.m3u*.

In a world where people with good vision and reading ability (and *really big* monitors) can't solve CAPTCHAs reliably, where black-hat hackers sell CAPTCHA crackers for spammers to create free email accounts, and where even the creator of the idea says it's begun to outlive its usefulness, what do

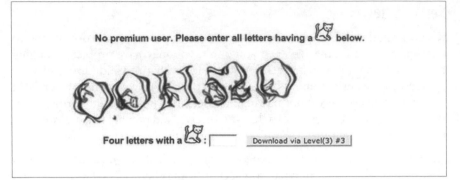

No premium user. Please enter all letters having a 🐱 below.

Four letters with a 🐱 : [＿＿＿] [Download via Level(3) #3]

Figure 5-3. Cat CAPTCHA (Source: http://flickr.com/photos/sebastiankippe/2459873043/)

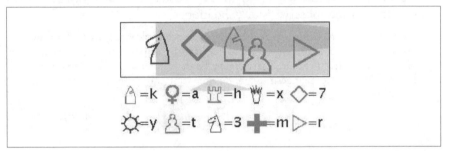

🔺=k ♀=a ♜=h 👑=x ◇=7

☼=y ♟=t ♞=3 ✚=m ▷=r

Figure 5-4. Chess CAPTCHA with key (Source: http://flickr.com/photos/cvander/2054028673/)

Figure 5-5. The answer must be under there somewhere (Source: http://flickr.com/photos/phygimus/2242915083/)

you think is happening? Surprisingly, in a lot of ways, it's actually getting worse. Visual verification schemes are getting such a bad rap that Flickr has hundreds of uploads featuring hilariously unsolvable puzzles, as shown in Figures 5-3 through 5-5.

Could you imagine trying to solve one of these on your mobile phone's display?

And some researchers have decided that the way to get themselves out of this hole is to keep digging. The latest approaches involve perceiving images, sometimes even in 3-D, that correspond to items like chairs and animals that we would recognize in real life. While researchers' creativity may be unparalleled, they are still trying to solve the wrong problem.

Avoid using CAPTCHAs. If you have a spam problem of any size, there are better, more inclusive solutions out there. When even those few very large sites have come to their senses regarding the use of these schemes and focused their energy elsewhere, we should all take the hint.

For a more complete anti-CAPTCHA rant, Matt wrote a paper titled "Inaccessibility of CAPTCHA: Alternatives to Visual Turing Tests on the Web,"* which outlines the strategies involved in finding an approach that more directly (and inclusively) addresses the problems that most people turn to visual verification to magically solve.

Jared Smith provides additional techniques in "Spam-free accessible forms" at *http://www.webaim.org/blog/spam_free_accessible_forms/*.

The Future of Forms

That's all there is for simple forms. Will it get any easier in the future? We hope so. In fact, in Chapter 9, we talk about two technologies that are already changing things for the better: Ajax and ARIA.

Summary

Use forms the way they were intended. If you use script, ensure that the form can be submitted without it. Avoid accesskeys, as they aren't very useful. Focus instead on simple code and use semantic HTML with CSS rather than layout tables wherever possible to present your content. Explicitly associate your form controls with their labels.

If you do find a legitimate type of control that you must use, a new set of rules will apply to ensure that your new component supports universal design. All this is covered in Chapters 8 and 9.

---

* Go to *http://www.w3.org/TR/turingtest/* to read his full article.

CHAPTER 6

Tabular Data

Have you ever found yourself at a train station in another country, unable to decipher the rows and columns of a train schedule? What information do you rely on to determine the departure platform? Departure time? Connections? This chapter is about ensuring that information is available without the spatial cues that tables provide.

When information about a data cell is *programmatically determinable*, software can extract and present the information in multiple ways. For example, you can generate a chart from a data table and vice versa. (See *http://www.wait -till-i.com/2008/01/08/generating-charts-from-accessible-data-tables-using-the -google-charts-api/* for an interesting take on the possibilities.) You can add a script that sorts or queries the table and provide a window into the data that can shrink, expand, or be spoken. In this chapter, we will discuss how to use tables to present data in a clean, reusable manner.

One thing to note as we begin: we do not discuss how to use tables for layout. These kinds of tables are of virtually no use to us in modern design now that CSS is widely supported. In fact, outside of HTML email, which is only beginning a long journey toward standards compliance, nearly any use of layout tables these days is unnecessary. As far as layout tables go, our advice is simple: don't use them.

Data Table Basics

The primary goal of marking up tables is to ensure that relationships between cells are *programmatically determinable*. The secondary goal is to ensure that the table can expand and contract with changes in screen size, font size, and text length, including minimizing horizontal scrolling on small screens. To meet these goals, do the following:

- Use th for row and column headings.
- Use td for data cells.
- Use td for cells that are both a heading and data.
- Split overly complicated tables into multiple simpler tables.
- Summarize navigation and orientation information.
- Use CSS to lay out interface objects.
- Don't nest tables.

Headings and Data

HTML has two elements for table cells: th and td. th indicates a row or column heading, whereas td marks the cell as data (td = table data, th = table heading). In some cases, a cell is both a heading and data (we'll talk more about that when we get into *complex tables*). Let's start with simple tables.

Simple tables generally have a one-to-many relationship between each heading and its children cells—in other words, no heading spans more than one column or row and none of its children are subheadings. The table shown in Figure 6-1 is a simple table because there is only one row of headings ("Attribute" and "Description") and each heading applies to all of the cells in its column.

Caption

A caption is a title—a short phrase that summarizes the contents of the table.

```
<table>
  <caption>Attributes highlighted in Universal
Design</caption>
    <tr>
      <th>Attribute</th>
      <th>Description</th>
    </tr>
    <tr>
      <td>summary</td>
      <td>description of the structure of a table</td>
    </tr>
    ...
    </tr>
</table>
```

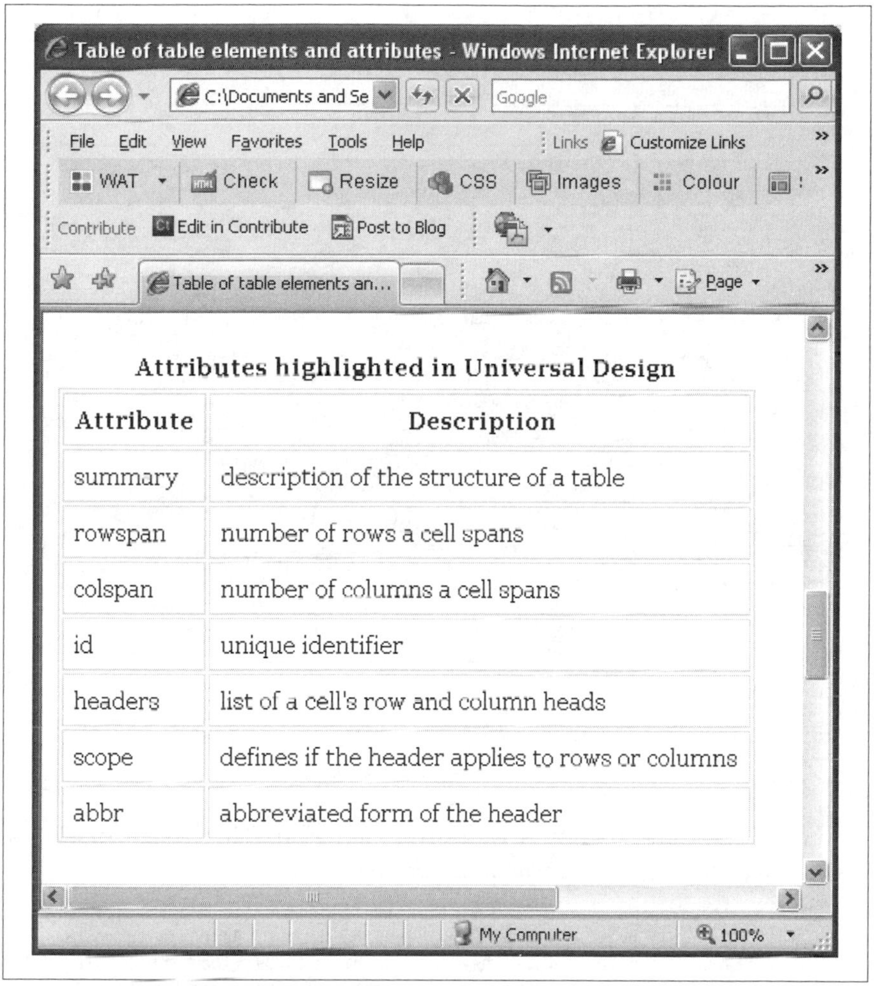

Table of table elements and attributes - Windows Internet Explorer

C:\Documents and Se   Google

File   Edit   View   Favorites   Tools   Help   Links   Customize Links

WAT   ▼   Check   Resize   CSS   Images   Colour

Contribute   Edit in Contribute   Post to Blog

Table of table elements an...   Page ▼

Attributes highlighted in Universal Design

Attribute	Description
summary	description of the structure of a table
rowspan	number of rows a cell spans
colspan	number of columns a cell spans
id	unique identifier
headers	list of a cell's row and column heads
scope	defines if the header applies to rows or columns
abbr	abbreviated form of the header

My Computer   100%

Figure 6-1. Example of a simple table

Complex Data Tables

A complex data table has at least one heading that spans multiple rows or columns. The table shown in Figure 6-2 (which was taken from *http://ks.water .usgs.gov/Kansas/pubs/fact-sheets/fs.024-00.pdf*) is a complex table because it has both row and column headings and several of the row headings span multiple rows. For example, "Flash Flood" applies to four rows—map numbers 21–24.

Significant Floods of the 20th Century

[M, million; B, billion]

Flood type	Map no.	Date	Area or stream with flooding	Reported deaths	Approximate cost (uninflated)	Comments
Regional flood	1	Mar.–Apr. 1913	Ohio, statewide	467	$143M	Excessive regional rain.
	2	Apr.–May 1927	Mississippi River from Missouri to Louisiana	unknown	$230M	Record discharge downstream from Cairo, Illinois.
	3	Mar. 1936	New England	150+	$300M	Excessive rainfall on snow.
	4	July 1951	Kansas and Neosho River Basins in Kansas	15	$800M	Excessive regional rain.
	5	Dec. 1964–Jan. 1965	Pacific Northwest	47	$430M	Excessive rainfall on snow.
	6	June 1965	South Platte and Arkansas Rivers in Colorado	24	$570M	14 inches of rain in a few hours in eastern Colorado.
	7	June 1972	Northeastern United States	117	$3.2B	Extratropical remnants of Hurricane Agnes.
	8	Apr.–June 1983 June 1983–1986	Shoreline of Great Salt Lake, Utah	unknown	$621M	In June 1986, the Great Salt Lake reached its highest elevation and caused $268M more in property damage.
	9	May 1983	Central and northeast Mississippi	1	$500M	Excessive regional rain.
	10	Nov. 1985	Shenandoah, James, and Roanoke Rivers in Virginia and West Virginia	69	$1.25B	Excessive regional rain.
	11	Apr. 1990	Trinity, Arkansas, and Red Rivers in Texas, Arkansas, and Oklahoma	17	$1B	Recurring intense thunderstorms.
	12	Jan. 1993	Gila, Salt, and Santa Cruz Rivers in Arizona	unknown	$400M	Persistent winter precipitation.
	13	May–Sept. 1993	Mississippi River Basin in central United States	48	$20B	Long period of excessive rainfall.
	14	May 1995	South-central United States	32	$5–6B	Rain from recurring thunderstorms.
	15	Jan.–Mar. 1995	California	27	$3B	Frequent winter storms.
	16	Feb. 1996	Pacific Northwest and western Montana	9	$1B	Torrential rains and snowmelt.
	17	Dec. 1996–Jan. 1997	Pacific Northwest and Montana	36	$2–3B	Torrential rains and snowmelt.
	18	Mar. 1997	Ohio River and tributaries	50+	$500M	Slow-moving frontal system.
	19	Apr.–May 1997	Red River of the North in North Dakota and Minnesota	8	$2B	Very rapid snowmelt.
	20	Sept. 1999	Eastern North Carolina	42	$6B	Slow-moving Hurricane Floyd.
Flash flood	21	June 14, 1903	Willow Creek in Oregon	225	unknown	City of Heppner, Oregon, destroyed.
	22	June 9–10, 1972	Rapid City, South Dakota	237	$160M	15 inches of rain in 5 hours.
	23	July 31, 1976	Big Thompson and Cache la Poudre Rivers in Colorado	144	$39M	Flash flood in canyon after excessive rainfall.
	24	July 19–20, 1977	Conemaugh River in Pennsylvania	78	$300M	12 inches of rain in 6–8 hours.
Ice-jam flood	25	May 1992	Yukon River in Alaska	0	unknown	100-year flood on Yukon River.
Storm-surge flood	26	Sept. 1900	Galveston, Texas	6,000+	unknown	Hurricane.
	27	Sept. 1938	Northeast United States	494	$306M	Hurricane.
	28	Aug. 1969	Gulf Coast, Mississippi and Louisiana	259	$1.4B	Hurricane Camille.
Dam-failure flood	29	Feb. 2, 1972	Buffalo Creek in West Virginia	125	$60M	Dam failure after excessive rainfall.
	30	June 5, 1976	Teton River in Idaho	11	$400M	Earthen dam breached.
	31	Nov. 8, 1977	Toccoa Creek in Georgia	39	$2.8M	Dam failure after excessive rainfall.
Mudflow	32	May 18, 1980	Toutle and lower Cowlitz Rivers in Washington	60	unknown	Result of eruption of Mt. St. Helens.

Figure 6-2. Example of a complex table

Summary

A well-written summary can provide a verbal map that helps someone using a screen reader navigate the data more efficiently:

```
<table summary=" The table is divided into six columns:  Map number,
  Date,  Area or stream with flooding, Reported deaths, Approximate costs
  (uninflated), and Comments.  The rows are grouped by flood types into six
  subcategories:  Regional flood, Flash flood, Ice-jam flood, Storm-surge
  flood, Dam-failure flood, and Mudflow flood.  ">
  ...
```

The preceding code summarizes the table with the following information:

- The number and titles of the column headings
- The stubhead ("The rows are...") and subheadings
- Key information

Most screen readers will announce the number of columns and rows upon entering a table. The summary attribute allows you to provide information about how to read the table—information that could be useful to anyone not familiar with the data you are presenting.

Always try to avoid using the same text in both the caption and the summary.

Specifying Relationships Between Data and Headings

In a complex data table, it isn't always programmatically obvious which headings apply to which cells. We can use the id and headers attributes to explicitly list all of the headings that apply to each data cell. First, assign each heading cell an id. Then, list the appropriate ids in the headers attribute of each data cell:

```
<tr>
  <th id="type">Flood Type</th>
  <th id="map">Map no.</th>
  <th id="date">Date</th>
  <th id="area">Area or stream with flooding</th>
  <th id="deaths">Reported deaths</th>
  <th id="cost">Approximate cost (uninflated)</th>
  <th id="comments">Comments</th>
</tr>
<tr>
  <td rowspan="5" id="regional">Regional flood</td>
  <td headers="regional map">1</td>
  <td headers="regional date">Mar.-Apr. 1913</td>
  <td headers="regional area">Ohio, statewide</td>
  <td headers="regional deaths">467</td>
  <td headers="regional cost">$143M</td>
  <td headers="regional comments">Excessive regional rain.</td>
</tr>
```

Depending on the screen reader and how it has been configured, the heading information will either be read all the time or only when it is "new." For example, someone may prefer to listen to column headings only when columns change—when reading horizontally across a row. Row and column numbers may or may not be read as well. Here are a few ways the cell "Ohio, statewide" may be read:

- Area with stream or flooding, Regional flood, Ohio, statewide
- Area with stream or flooding, Regional flood, Ohio, statewide
- Row 2, column 4, Area with stream or flooding, Ohio, statewide
- Regional flood, Ohio, statewide

You can combine techniques such that the rows with rowspan use the headers attribute and row headings that don't span multiple rows only use the th element. For example, the following is the markup for the last row of the table for which there is only one entry (one row). Thus, there is no rowspan, no id, and no headers. However, since "Mudflow flood" is both data and a row heading, it is marked with a td (rather than th). To indicate that it is a heading and to clarify that it applies to the row, the scope is set to "row."

```
<tr>
    <td scope="row">Mudflow flood</td>
    <td>32</td>
    <td>May 18, 1980</td>
    <td>Toutle and lower Cowlitz Rivers in Washington</td>
    <td>60</td>
    <td>unknown</td>
    <td>Result of eruption of Mt. St. Helens.</td>
</tr>
```

Specifying relationships—another approach

A second approach, yet less consistently supported by assistive technologies, is to group related rows and associate a heading with the scope attribute. It is more elegant, and we hope it gains support in the future.

This technique uses the rowspan and scope attributes. rowspan is used to indicate how many rows a heading applies to, while scope indicates that the heading applies to the row.

```
<tr>
    <th rowspan="5" scope="row">Regional flood</th>
    <td>1</td>
    <td>Mar.-Apr. 1913</td>
    <td>Ohio, statewide</td>
    <td>467</td>
    <td>$143M</td>
    <td>Excessive regional rain.</td>
</tr>
<tr>
    <td>2</td>
    <td>Apr.-May 1927</td>
    <td>Mississippi River from Missouri to Louisiana</td>
    <td>unknown</td>
    <td>$230M</td>
    <td>Record discharge downstream from Cairo, Illinois.</td>
</tr>
<tr>
    <td>3</td>
    <td>Mar. 1936</td>
    <td>New England</td>
    <td>150+</td>
    <td>$300M</td>
    <td>Excessive rainfall on snow.</td>
</tr>
<tr>
    <td>4</td>
    <td>July 1951</td>
    <td>Kansas and Neosho River Basins in Kansas</td>
```

```
    <td>15</td>
    <td>$800M</td>
    <td>Excessive regional rain.</td>
</tr>
<tr>
    <td>5</td>
    <td>Dec. 1964 - Jan. 1965</td>
    <td>Pacific Northwest</td>
    <td>47</td>
    <td>$430M</td>
    <td>Excessive rainfall on snow.</td>
</tr>
```

Readability, Layout, and Design

Depending on how much data you are displaying, you may want to tweak the visual design to ease reading. Assuming you've read this far and you've provided the necessary HTML framework for your data, you can easily change cell colors, padding, margin, and borders to make the data easier to read.

5:27	5:40	5:45	5:49	5:53	5:56	6:01	6:05	6:12	6:14	6:16	6:17	6:20	6:22	6:25	6:27	6:31
5:42	5:55	6:00	6:04	6:08	6:11	6:16	6:20	6:27	6:29	6:31	6:32	6:35	6:37	6:40	6:42	6:46
5:57	6:10	6:15	6:19	6:23	6:26	6:31	6:35	6:42	6:44	6:40	6:47	6:50	6:52	6:55	0:57	7:01
6:12	6:25	6:30	6:34	6:38	6:41	6:46	6:50	6:57	6:59	7:01	7:02	7:05	7:07	7:10	7:12	7:16
6:27	6:40	6:45	6:49	6:53	6:56	7:01	7:05	7:12	7:14	7:16	7:17	7:20	7:22	7:25	7:27	7:31
6:42	6:55	7:00	7:04	7:08	7:11	7:16	7:20	7:27	7:29	7:31	7:32	7:35	7:37	7:40	7:42	7:46
6:57	7:10	7:15	7:19	7:23	7:26	7:31	7:35	7:42	7:44	7:46	7:47	7:50	7:52	7:55	7:57	8:01
7:12	7:25	7:30	7:34	7:38	7:41	7:46	7:50	7:57	7:59	8:01	8:02	8:05	8:07	8:10	8:12	8:16
7:27	7:40	7:45	7:49	7:53	7:56	8:01	8:05	8:12	8:14	8:16	8:17	8:20	8:22	8:25	8:27	8:31
7:42	7:55	8:00	8:04	8:08	8:11	8:16	8:20	8:27	8:29	8:31	8:32	8:35	8:37	8:40	8:42	8:46
7:57	8:10	8:15	8:19	8:23	8:26	8:31	8:35	8:42	8:44	8:46	0:47	8:50	8:52	8:55	8:57	9:01
8:12	8:25	8:30	8:34	8:38	8:41	8:46	8:50	8:57	8:59	9:01	9:02	9:05	9:07	9:10	9:12	9:16
8:27	8:40	8:45	8:49	8:53	8:56	9:01	9:05	9:12	9:14	9:16	9:17	9:20	9:22	9:25	0:27	9:31
8:42	8:55	9:00	9:04	9:08	9:11	9:16	9:20	9:27	9:29	9:31	9:32	9:35	9:37	9:40	9:42	9:46
8:57	9:10	9:15	9:19	9:23	9:26	9:31	9:35	9:42	9:44	9:46	9:47	9:50	9:52	9:55	9:57	10:01
9:12	9:25	9:30	9:34	9:38	9:41	9:46	9:50	9:57	9:59	10:01	10:02	10:05	10:07	10:10	10:12	10:16

Figure 6-3. Bus schedule, where blue indicates bikes are not allowed…at least onscreen; the blue disappears in black and white and the information that should be conveyed is lost—another reason additional coding measures are needed

Color

Color is a beautiful thing. We encourage the use of "zebra-striping"—coloring every other row—to make a table easier to read. However, we do discourage the use of color to provide important information. Figure 6-3 shows a bus schedule (from *http://bart.gov/stations/schedules/lineSchedules_ROUTE11 _WD.asp*) with several cells shaded blue, indicating bikes aren't allowed on the bus at those times.

If someone is not perceiving color—either because of low contrast on a mobile phone or because he is using a screen reader—he will not have access to that important information. Instead, use an abbreviation like "NB" or an icon with alt text that conveys "no bikes."

Adding an asterisk to each cell provides a nonvisual indicator:

```
<td class="nobike">*6:27</td>
```

Another option is an image with a text equivalent:

```
<td class="nobike"><img src="no-bike.gif" alt="no bikes"/>6:27</td>
```

Footnotes and Keys

Provide a means for people to find and decipher keys and footnotes. This is useful for people who may not be able to glance at the key, understand what it means, find what it means, or remember what it means. Let's look at some examples.

Use the `abbr` element with the `title` attribute:

```
<td class="nobike">6:27 <abbr title="no bike">nb</abbr></td>
```

Put the key in a `div` before the table and link to it from an asterisk in the table:

```
<div id="key"><p>Blue cells with an asterisk indicate routes that do
not allow bikes</p></div>
...
<td class="nobike">6:27 <a href="#key">*</a></td>
```

CSS

We've mentioned before that tables are not for layout. If your authoring tool is generating tables instead of CSS, it's time to upgrade. For more information on how to lay out graphics, multimedia, forms, or other interface components, read Chapter 4. However, using CSS to style a table of data is extremely helpful.

The primary difference between the default presentation of `td` and `th` is that `th` is a heavier font weight and is centered vertically and horizontally, whereas `td` is normal font weight, left-aligned (in left-to-right languages), and centered vertically.

Padding

The default for most browsers is not to provide much padding. To open up the space in each cell, add top, left, and bottom padding. In the following example, we use pixels to ensure that if the text size increases, the padding stays the same—giving the text more room to flow:

```
th, td {padding-bottom: 10px; padding-left: 10px;
padding-right: 10px;}
```

Column widths

Specify column widths in em or percent so that the table can resize proportionally if text size changes or word length changes with translation.

```
th, td {width: 2em;}
```

Borders

Don't separate columns with a character, such as the following:

```
<td class="td1">|</td>
```

You get the same effect with:

```
td {border-top: none; border-bottom: none; border-left: solid;
border-right: solid;}.
```

pre

Never use pre to lay out data. We didn't think we had to say it, but there is an unfortunate number of sites that use pre instead of table markup, including a major metropolitan bus system that lays out its pages in nested tables, then stuffs entire timetables into a single pre. Using pre means throwing away semantics and styling capabilities. The point is to make the data come alive, not to kill it off completely.

Summary

When used properly—that is, when used to present data—tables are a good thing. You're providing an easy way for people to make comparisons. Marking up tables for universal design ensures that when accessed via a mobile device, a small screen, or with a screen reader, those comparisons can still be made because you've identified the relationships between the cells.

Video and Audio

In 2005, Web 2.0 gained a new standard-bearer. It was based in hot new technology, attracted people and venture capital dollars, and above all, it was viral. Centers for Disease Control and Prevention viral.

And yet, the technology that drove this company wasn't Ajax. What made YouTube an instant hit was web video. YouTube took advantage of the video functionality found in Flash Player, not to mention gigabits of bandwidth, to deliver one of the most addictive experiences on the Web.

If you're looking to be the next YouTube, this book won't help you. In fact, maybe nothing will, unless you're a CEO of a Fortune 100 company and you're looking to unload a few billion dollars on hosting, content monitoring and filtering, and defending against international regulatory and civil actions. But video is now a first-class citizen of the modern Web, and everyone from designers to developers to marketing departments to educators should understand when, how, and why to use it.

Web Video: The Early Years

Though video on the Web came into its own only within the last few years, computing and video have a long history. If you know a former Amiga owner, this will be obvious to you, as they will have described its role in vivid, excruciating detail. From the release of the Amiga 1000 in 1985, it was one of the premier tools for editing video in production environments. However, in those days, a 7 MHz Motorola 68000 processor wasn't quite up to the task of processing 525 interlaced lines; the system offered only overlaid graphics and control over external videotape recorders (VTRs).

The first mass-market video application was QuickTime, which debuted in 1991. Used primarily in "multimedia" CDs, QuickTime videos were often chiclet-sized 160x120 movies, to accommodate the slow CPUs and low-resolution displays of the day. (By way of comparison, the iPhone and iPod touch could display 8 of those 160x120 movies simultaneously on their 480x320 display. The iPhone's 620 MHz ARM CPU and 16 GB of storage wouldn't have been anything to sneeze at in 1991, either.) Still, in applications such as educational materials, video in any form was a huge step forward for what was mostly a text-centric medium.

While the Web was still taking shape, small numbers of users had begun working with video online. They were divided into two constituencies: the Usenet file sharers, perhaps best known as the folks who popularized MP3s; and the video chatters, using early programs such as CU-SeeMe to connect with one another. The Usenet alt.binaries groups experimented with a few different formats, but, early on at least, most settled on some variant of the Motion Picture Experts Group's MPEG-1 format. Mind you, back then, you needed a lot of things to be able to watch anything good: a high-quality Usenet newsreader application—which could read multipart, uuencoded messages and decode them automatically—as well as a set of codecs, a player application, and all the time in the world, as these huge videos came down over 14.4 kbps or 28.8 kbps modems. YouTube, it wasn't. But it did, along with live video chat technology, lay the groundwork for the next wave of applications to take the technology mainstream.

Real Networks released the RealVideo player in 1997. Already popular for introducing streaming radio with its RealAudio format, Real's first step into video codecs made live net video a reality. It would take a number of years before these technologies were used frequently, but by the early 2000s, most major media outlets worldwide were producing either simulcast or recorded streams of their content via the Web, using the Real, QuickTime, or Microsoft Windows Media formats.

The next change in the landscape came in 2002 with the addition of video capability in Macromedia Flash Player 6. (Macromedia was subsequently purchased by Adobe in 2005.) Flash was already widely deployed, enjoying more installs than any of the existing video plug-ins, and as its installed base upgraded to newer versions, Flash quickly had an impact on the video market.

Suddenly, the potential for web video had increased. Flash, which had evolved from a platform for animation into a reasonably full-featured multimedia platform, was now capable not only of integrating video but also of overlaying and synchronizing that video with other graphics. Designers reacted tentatively at first to the addition of video; it would take at least a couple more years for most Flash projects to contemplate planning a shoot, producing a final package, and hosting large video files for their clients.

Then came the rise of YouTube. YouTube was not the first aggregator of small clips of web video: Real, Microsoft, and Apple had offered free content to users through their respective players. Real even offered its paid RealOne service to provide more streams at higher quality. But the walled-garden approach each provider took meant users were limited to what was in each company's directory and were strongly persuaded to use the player application to find that content, leaving them little opportunity to share that content with others. With Flash video, on the other hand, the browser *was* the player, and user-generated content was easy to find. In fact, by reducing a video producer's hosting costs to zero (or even paying them a cut of advertising revenue, as Revver did, with YouTube following), the web video sites fundamentally solved one of the biggest barriers to the proliferation of video content.

What may be the final piece to the puzzle (at least for now) is high-definition, or HD, content. The vast majority of the content published to the Web has been at a lower resolution than that of standard-definition television. But HD capabilities exploded onto the scene in 2007, thanks to the rollout of the H.264 codec and an arms race between Adobe, Microsoft, and Apple. H.264 (also known as MPEG-4 AVC, for Advanced Video Coding) is a video compression standard that offers high-quality, high-resolution video with relatively low bandwidth requirements. In other words, H.264 is the silver bullet for HD over the Web. Apple was the first to release major player support for H.264, integrating it into QuickTime, and by extension iTunes. It also built support into the fifth-generation iPod, and H.264 has been the underlying technology for the video content available for sale via iTunes.

The next move was Microsoft's. The first preview release of Silverlight included support for Windows Media videos up to a resolution of 720p (1280x720). Adobe soon thereafter released a version of Flash Player with a codec for H.264 and support for Full HD, or 1080p (1920x1080) resolution. Given that no broadcast network has even begun transmitting in 1080p, this effectively marks the end of the resolution debate until standards and content for the upcoming 2160- and 4320-line specifications start to appear, which is several years off from the time of this book's publication.

Video and Universal Design

It's important for content creators to understand the history of video because it all comes down to four issues that constantly need to be watched:

- Bandwidth
- CPU usage
- Screen resolution
- Player support

Table 7-1 lays out some of the technologies we talked about to give you a better idea of what we know. QuickTime, when it was first released, enjoyed more bandwidth for its content than any other technology we listed for at least the next 10 years, as most QuickTime content was served up at 150–300KB/s (or, in networking terms, 1.2–2.4Mbit/s). But it was still shackled by CPU power and an audience that was just in the process of moving up from VGA (640x480). It was also virtually the only game in town, so player support was hardly a consideration. Real's first video player had better CPUs to rely on and a healthy 1024x768 on many displays, but Internet bandwidth was still on the order of 28.8 kbps to 56 kbps on the vast majority of clients, and Real's content was still proprietary.

Table 7-1. Overview of differences between video formats

	Bandwidth	CPU	Output Quality	Player support
QuickTime 1.0	High	Very low	Low	Very low
RealVideo 1.0	Very low	Low	Moderate	Very low
MPEG-1	Low	Low	Moderate	High
MPEG-4	Low	Moderate	High	Very high
H.264	Low	High	Very high	High

All three major players (iTunes, Silverlight, and Flash Player) support full-screen viewing.

Codecs are codecs are codecs. They come around. People argue about them. They get poor implementations, then pretty decent ones, and the content flows from there. But H.264 broke the mold, going from zero to near-complete support in the industry in an extremely short period of time. A properly encoded H.264 video can be played in QuickTime (and therefore iTunes), RealPlayer, or Flash, at HD-quality resolutions, and on the iPod at 640x480. It also offers a high degree of compression, which means less of a hit on bandwidth.

Optimizing Web Video

So, what's the catch? High compression means more CPU cycles are needed to decode a stream. That means older machines, as well as most devices, may struggle to play back larger H.264-encoded files. Usually, players will respond to an overflow of data by "dropping" frames in the playback. This is considered bad form, as it results in a jerky visual appearance at best, and irritating distortion or choppy audio can also occur. If you're just playing back a small 320x240 video, it won't matter much if you use MPEG-4 or H.264, but as files get larger, the CPU-versus-bandwidth debate can become significant.

As video becomes a more central feature, though, a single format or size won't be enough to satisfy every user, making a dedicated video server more and more of a necessity. Many video server products can perform on-the-fly transcoding of source material and content negotiation to determine which format and bit rate is the best for the current user. A Windows Media client could receive an HD stream in WMV-HD format, for example, while someone on a mobile phone could get a 20 kbps feed in mobile-friendly 3GPP.

Accessibility in Video

If you've been paying attention so far, you may be afraid to hear the accessibility story for web video. Don't be! It's actually not that bad, considering. All of the major players—QuickTime, Windows Media, RealPlayer, and Flash Player—support captioning. In fact, captioning is so well supported that there are scads of different formats to choose from!

Oh, wait. That's not a good thing. But it could be a lot worse.

The reason captioning is such a mature technology is simple: it's been around for decades. *The French Chef*, in 1971, was the first program to be "open-captioned," meaning that captions were overlaid on (or "burned into") the source so that all viewers could see them. *The Captioned ABC News*, which was also open-captioned, made its debut in 1973. The closed captioning system, made official in 1980, uses extra bandwidth in the TV signal to send a captioning signal, which is decoded by a receiver, that used to be a set-top box intended for deaf and hard-of-hearing users. But by 1993, closed captioning decoders were required on all televisions 13" and larger. These days, it's nearly impossible to find someone who hasn't seen captions, if only on the screen at her local sports bar.

Captioning often gets conflated with two similar terms, so let's get them straight here:

Transcripts
> Word-for-word copies of what was spoken. They may also contain audio or visual cues, such that the transcript itself makes sense without the source material. Transcripts are not synchronized with video.

Subtitles

Synchronized chunks of text, used to translate the spoken content into another language. Since they are designed for translation rather than for deaf or hard-of-hearing users, they contain no text equivalents for sounds.

Captions

Synchronized chunks of text, optimized for deaf and hard-of-hearing viewers. Unlike transcripts, they may not contain exactly what speakers have said, but may be contracted for clear, easy reading. Important sound cues (known in the captioning trade as "nonspoken information") are also included in captions. (In the UK, however, captions are not differentiated; both forms are known as "subtitles.")

It's possible to write an entire book on captioning—in fact, many authors already have. And if you have a small amount of recorded content you want to caption by yourself, you can do a reasonably good job using a free tool called MAGpie (which we discuss in the next section). On the other hand, if you have, say, 10,000 hours of video archives, or you need to be able to caption live content in real time (quite a feat by itself), you will need to call in the cavalry. Several companies offer various kinds of captioning services, at varied rates.

On the Web, many of the rules for captioning are the same as they are for TV: small chunks of text, displayed at a reasonable rate, with important sounds also captioned. What is different, though, is how they're distributed. A few formats support caption data as part of the video stream so that viewers receive the video and caption data all in one file. But it is much more common for caption files to be saved to a supported format, with timecodes to synchronize them with the video content. This requires one or more external files to be loaded, which is easier for authors, but can result in captions being lost in the shuffle.

In August 2008, YouTube joined its sister site Google Video in offering support for "captions and subtitles," using the SubViewer (.SUB) and SubRip (.SRT) formats, commonly used for foreign movie subtitling. You can assemble your captions in these formats, which are very simple text files associating timecodes with the text to be displayed, and upload them to the YouTube or Google Video page for your video. The captions will then be available in a Closed Captioning menu inside the YouTube Flash player. Note, however, that users of other players, such as the YouTube iPhone application, will not see those captions or subtitles.

Most modern captioning formats use markup. QuickTime and RealPlayer support captions done in the W3C SMIL (pronounced "smile") format. Microsoft's captioning format, SAMI (pronounced "sammy"), is more like

HTML. Flash supports W3C's DFXP format, better known as Timed Text. (QuickTime also supports captions embedded as metadata in H.264 files.)

Captioning Your Video

A number of tools are available to make sense of this mishmash of standards. Perhaps the most popular of these are the free tools produced by the National Center for Accessible Media (NCAM) at WGBH-TV in Boston. Their MAGpie product, available for both Windows and Mac OS X, allows authors to caption their own media and export those captions in any of the most popular formats. We're going to demonstrate how to create a caption file for QuickTime and Flash using this tool.

Here's a video Matt made in 2005, titled "A Podcasting How-To" (see Figure 7-1):

http://www.archive.org/download/podcasthowto/podcasthowto.mp4

If you want to follow along, you can download MAGpie from the NCAM site at:

http://ncam.wgbh.org/webaccess/magpie/

Once MAGpie is running, we will select our video file as the input. Let's save time and use this file as our input:

http://www.archive.org/download/podcasthowto/podcasthowto.en-US.qt .txt

This caption file, which was output by MAGpie, is a simple text file with some timecodes:

```
{QTtext}{timescale:100}{font:Trebuchet MS}{size:14}
{backColor:0,0,0} {textColor:65535,65535,65535}{width:320}{justify:center}

[00:00:00.00]
Hi folks, my name is Matt May and I do Staccato.

[00:00:03.97]
It's a Creative Commons music show.

[00:00:06.30]
I've had a lot of people that have been asking me,

[00:00:08.47]
how do you do the show? What's your equipment?

[00:00:11.14]
How do you put the show together?
(...)
```

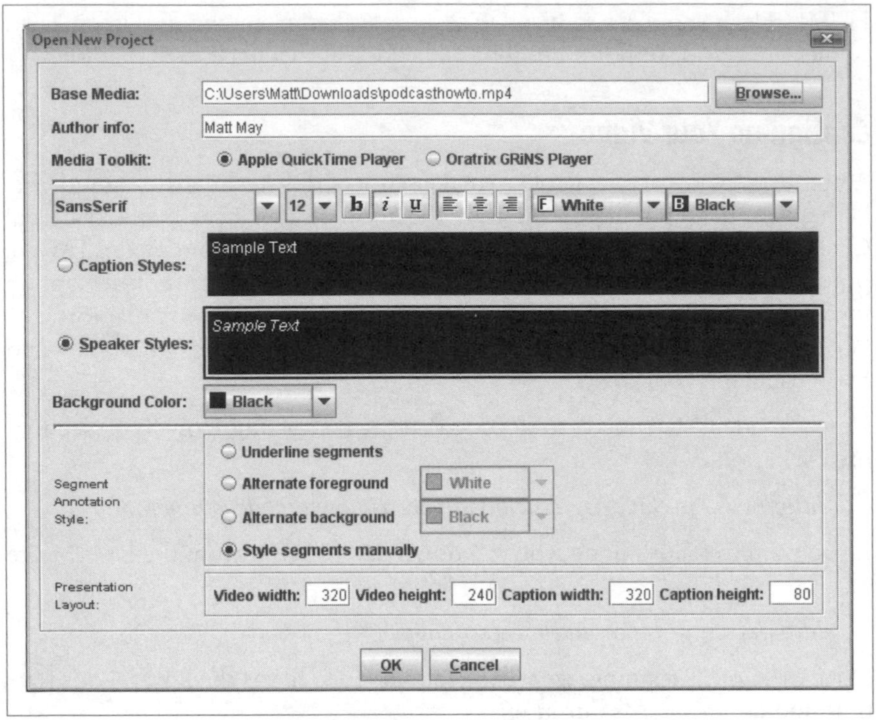

Open New Project

Base Media: `C:\Users\Matt\Downloads\podcasthowto.mp4` Browse...

Author info: `Matt May`

Media Toolkit: ● Apple QuickTime Player ○ Oratrix GRiNS Player

SansSerif ▼ | 12 ▼ | **b** *i* u | ☰ ☰ ☰ | F White ▼ | B Black ▼

○ Caption Styles:
> Sample Text

● Speaker Styles:
> *Sample Text*

Background Color: ■ Black ▼

Segment Annotation Style:
○ Underline segments
○ Alternate foreground — ■ White ▼
○ Alternate background — ■ Black ▼
● Style segments manually

Presentation Layout: Video width: `320` Video height: `240` Caption width: `320` Caption height: `80`

OK   Cancel

Figure 7-1. MAGpie project window

We can import this into our project by going to the Tracks menu and selecting Import Track. Then browse for the caption file, and select the radio button marked "QTtext", as this is a QuickTime-formatted caption file. The captions will appear in a screen of their own, with the video shown on another panel. See Figure 7-2.

MAGpie has a navigation panel at the top of the screen, which contains a stop button, pause, plus and minus controls to move back and forth between the captions, and three play buttons, which correspond to slow motion, regular speed, and fast forward. Some helpful keystrokes include:

F6
> Play or pause file

F9
> Mark the selected caption's start time with the current timestamp from the file

F10
> Mark the selected caption's end time with the current timestamp from the file

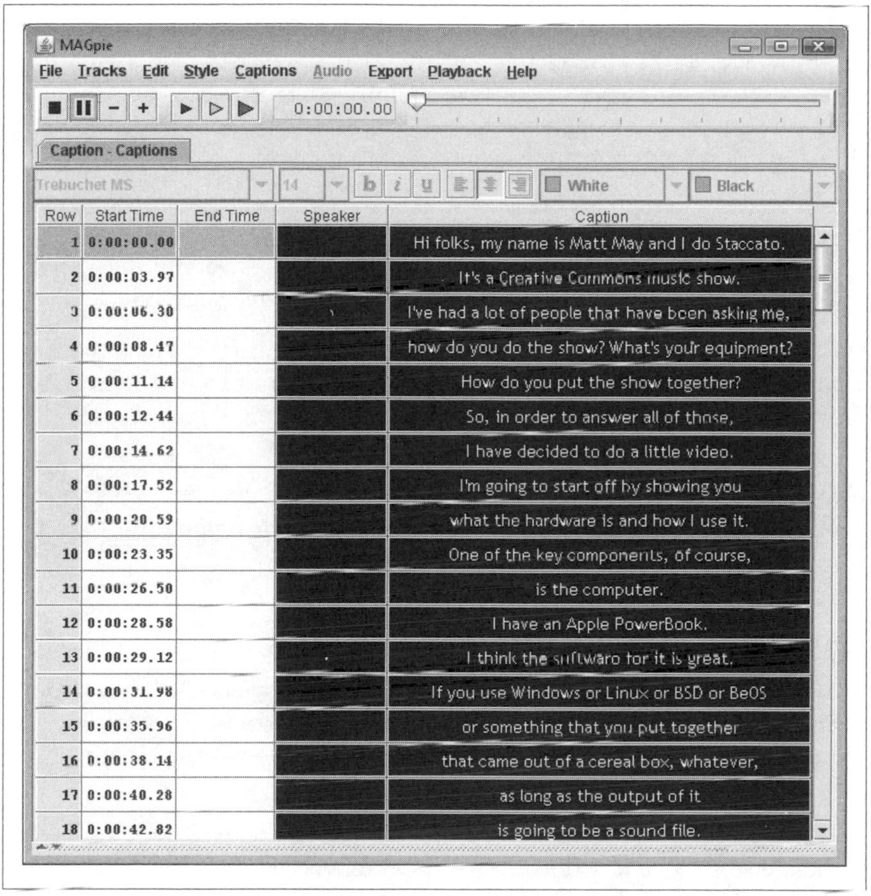
MAGpie
File Tracks Edit Style Captions Audio Export Playback Help
0:00:00.00
Caption - Captions
Trebuchet MS
14
White
Black
Row
Start Time
End Time
Speaker
Caption
1 0:00:00.00 Hi folks, my name is Matt May and I do Staccato.
2 0:00:03.97 It's a Creative Commons music show.
3 0:00:06.30 I've had a lot of people that have been asking me,
4 0:00:08.47 how do you do the show? What's your equipment?
5 0:00:11.14 How do you put the show together?
6 0:00:12.44 So, in order to answer all of those,
7 0:00:14.62 I have decided to do a little video.
8 0:00:17.52 I'm going to start off by showing you
9 0:00:20.59 what the hardware is and how I use it.
10 0:00:23.35 One of the key components, of course,
11 0:00:26.50 is the computer.
12 0:00:28.58 I have an Apple PowerBook.
13 0:00:29.12 I think the software for it is great.
14 0:00:31.98 If you use Windows or Linux or BSD or BeOS
15 0:00:35.96 or something that you put together
16 0:00:38.14 that came out of a cereal box, whatever,
17 0:00:40.28 as long as the output of it
18 0:00:42.82 is going to be a sound file.

Figure 7-2. MAGpie captioning interface

You may feel more comfortable transcribing a video in one pass, and then syncing it with the source in a second pass. If that's the case, importing a plain-text file of the transcript into MAGpie is a good start. Then you can hit F9 to mark caption changes.

Hiring a Captioner

If you don't have the time or energy to do the captioning yourself, you have a few options. For live events, Caption Colorado offers real-time captioning in every major streaming format. The company specializes in captioning for financial reporting, online learning, and teleconferences. You should be aware that real-time captioners are highly trained professionals and should expect to pay something on the order of $5 per minute for live captioning.

Captioning or transcribing recorded content is much easier and somewhat less expensive. You also have many more options available to you. For example, at the low end, you can use a service such as CastingWords, which will produce a transcript for as little as 75 cents per minute—that is, if you can wait up to a month for it to be done. Overnight service costs $2.50 per minute. Casting-Words will also add timestamps for 10 cents a minute.

Automated captioning services are also available and can be more economical. AutomaticSync offers one such service, which will do voice recognition-based captioning in all major formats, including podcasts. They will do the transcription for you, or sync a transcript you provide to the source video.

DocSoft offers an industrial-strength approach: they'll sell you a rack-mounted server loaded with software that will mine your audio and video content, and provide it in an assortment of different formats. Among their target markets are education and broadcasting.

If you have more specific needs, or want to find all the qualified companies in your vicinity, the Closed Captioning website (*http://captions.org*) lets you search companies by service and location.

Audio Description

MAGpie also lets you add audio descriptions to your video. While audio descriptions are harder to do well, they are necessary in a number of cases to give blind and low-vision users the information they need to keep up with what's going on.

To get some idea of what audio descriptions sound like, we have two recommendations: go to a described movie, or watch an episode of *The Simpsons* with your TV's SAP function on. (Don't you wish your teachers gave you homework like that?) The Descriptive Video Service is another product of MAGpie's creators at WGBH, and they describe a number of movies and TV shows. You can see which movies currently in theaters are described at *http:// ncam.wgbh.org/mopix/*.

You can listen to the DVS track by asking for a headset at the theater. Action films are highly recommended. (It may have been the only thing that made *The Matrix Reloaded* worth watching.) For the full accessible experience, you could also ask for a visor, which sits in a cup holder, enabling you to see the reflected captioning stream in the back of the theater. This feature, called Rear Window Captioning, allows deaf and hard-of-hearing people to watch movies alongside their hearing friends.

With podcasting video, there is really no reason for audio description because all of the content that's presented visually is also spoken at some point in the video. For example, as Matt points out the features of his studio in "A Podcasting How-To," he describes them in turn, so an audio description track would only add redundancy. But if anything in the scene is meaningful, such as the setting, or a voiceover doesn't adequately describe the action on the screen, audio descriptions can be used to fill in the gaps for blind and low-vision users.

The application of audio descriptions is truly an art form. Depending on the source material, it can require substantial amounts of content to be communicated in brief pauses in the main audio track. In order to do this, it may at times be necessary not only to prepare concise descriptions of what is happening on the screen but to leave enough silence in the main track to allow those descriptions to be inserted. In general, if you control the production of the source material, it's best to keep in mind that what you're communicating onscreen needs to have an auditory equivalent at some point, and if that's not possible, there has to be enough silence for an audio description to do the heavy lifting.

Accessible Mobile Video

Mobile devices that are capable of displaying video generally don't have enough horsepower left over to even contemplate captions. They are also usually limited by small displays and low resolution. Captions aren't particularly viable on a 128x96 display.

Another issue is the lack of a single standard for captioned online content. Closed captioning on analog television is a universal design solution, since nearly all receivers can understand it. But as we've seen in this chapter, the standards for captioning video streams are all over the map, which doesn't bode well for support in devices. The iPhone and newer video-capable iPods can display captions embedded in H.264 files, and other devices have players that support SubRip or other open standards for subtitling, but we can't recommend one single method to caption all content in a manner that will work for a wide array of video-capable devices.

The only solution that will work for mobile captioning would be open-captioned content. This would mean that all viewers of your content would see captions. If you decide to go this route, you will need to select a font that will display clearly against bright and dark backgrounds and will be readable at very low resolutions. (Think about reading captions on a flip phone.) Use sans-serif fonts, in a high-contrast color such as yellow, and test the output on as many devices as you can.

As video-capable devices continue to be commoditized, we will see more and more that support captions natively, and we can only hope that device manufacturers understand the benefits that come with a single captioning standard. Until that occurs, there are no good solutions that incorporate universal design into mobile video. The best we can offer for this is a text transcript.

Transcripts and Text Alternatives

Given what is required in terms of time and or money to produce captioned content, it's sometimes necessary to provide a text transcript of video content. And in the case of audio, transcripts are the only way to associate a text equivalent. Transcripts are a basic requirement for meeting WCAG 2 with prerecorded media. It's also the best first step for creating synchronized captions.

In fact, if you've scripted your audio segments beforehand, there's virtually no work necessary to it. Just upload your script, edited for any ad-libbed material. The bonus here is that you've just made your video more searchable. Very few search engines to date have done anything with video, so text is still the lingua franca.

Summary

It can take some time to produce quality web video that can be used across browsers, devices, and disability categories. Ultimately, though, making the decisions necessary to select a standard format, such as MPEG-4 or H.264, or to go with a server that outputs in many formats, will leave you in a solid position as web video continues its rapid evolution.

Likewise, captioning has benefits that affect a large cross-section of the Web. According to the National Institutes of Health, 12% of all Americans—a staggering 36.4 million—have some kind of hearing trouble. And that's before we add in situational disabilities, such as noisy environments, office PCs that come without speakers, or people who simply don't like being distracted by audio. Caption files and transcripts are also plain text, which makes them searchable, and while search engines still struggle to find a strategy to index audio and video content, this also works to your advantage.

 For an example of a video search engine, check out the DO-IT Video Search at *http://www.washington.edu/doit/Video/Search/*.

Audio descriptions aren't as universally beneficial, but for the group of people who need them, they arc indispensable. Still, it's best to keep in mind the need for spoken confirmation of what's going on as you produce video content, so that the amount you need to describe in order to be reasonably accessible is minimal.

Scripting

We know what happened the first time HTML was stretched beyond its limits: spacer GIFs, nested layout tables, font tags, "best viewed in my browser" badges, and fragmented standards. And worst of all, poorly trained content creators, whose limited knowledge of how things ought to be continues to plague us almost 15 years later.

What we have learned is that no language will be ideal for all possible uses. HTML is a *fantastic* format for rich-text documents. And we've learned how to layer it with CSS and script to make it a pretty good platform for application frontends. We've even added an object called `XmlHttpRequest`, named the combination Ajax, and its phenomenal spread is the topic of dozens of books of its own.

Ajax is just one of a growing number of pretty good UI platforms, each of them well-suited to the modern Web. They're fast, functional, and cross-platform.

Now, here's the catch: whether you're developing with Ajax, Adobe's Flash and Flex, Microsoft's Silverlight, or any other web-based platform, your responsibilities go beyond web accessibility and into the world of software accessibility. Some of the rules change when dealing with software, and in the next two chapters, we explain what these new rules entail. We also show you what rules from HTML still apply.

Building on a Solid Foundation

> Progressive enhancement uses web technologies in a layered fashion that allows everyone to access the basic content and functionality of a web page, using any browser or Internet connection, while also providing those with better bandwidth or more advanced browser software an enhanced version of the page.[*]
>
> —Wikipedia, "Progressive Enhancement" (retrieved September 2, 2008)

> The key word here, I think, is unobtrusive. DHTML of this kind should just drop into place, providing a better user experience for people whose browsers can support it, and *not affecting* those whose browsers cannot.[†]
>
> —Stuart Langridge, November 2002

Progressive enhancement is a framework; *Unobtrusive JavaScript* is applying the framework to JavaScript-based applications, and it represents a growing body of best practices. You may be asking yourself, "Is it possible to use Java-Script as an enhancement rather than a necessity? And even if it is, why would I?" Answers: Yes, it's possible. Why would you? Well...

1996 was a landmark year in web history: Netscape introduced JavaScript (as "Mocha" and then "LiveScript") as the nonprogrammer's alternative to Java, at the end of 1995. Microsoft released a JavaScript dialect called JScript in August 1996—alongside a Visual Basic-like language called VBScript. That same year, the W3C published CSS1 as a W3C Recommendation. For the next few years, using scripting and styling was an exercise in translation and redundancy.

In 1998, things started looking up—folks agreed on ECMAScript and the DOM Level 1 was published as a W3C Recommendation. Scripting was starting to coalesce, but CSS was still broken. It would take another two years (plus lots of work by the Web Standards Project and the rise of the Opera browser) before browsers found common ground. However, there is still work to be done. Today, in 2008—*12 years* after the publication of CSS1, and 10 years after CSS2—you will still find many differences in support between browsers.

Looking back through this same time frame from the perspective of someone using a screen reader in 1996, we didn't find many problems caused by scripts; few sites were using them, and they were still relatively rudimentary. By 1998, we had identified most of the major issues with scripts, which continue to exist today (see "Page Author Guidelines Version 8"—*http://trace.wisc.edu/archive/html_guidelines/central.htm#SCRIPT.Script*). At the time, the only recommendations for making scripts accessible were to provide text alternatives, either

---

[*] *http://en.wikipedia.org/wiki/Progressive_enhancement*

[†] *http://www.kryogenix.org/code/browser/aqlists/*

---

through text-only versions of sites or using the `noscript` element. There wasn't any major progress in making scripts accessible until WAI issued the DHTML roadmap in 2005, which has evolved into a series of documents that outline the Accessible Rich Internet Applications specification, or WAI-ARIA.

Now, if we look at the development of mobile devices, there are more browsers available today than ever before, and the number is growing, as are the differences among them. Developers are encouraged to debug and test code in as many browsers as possible. With the wide array of devices and device capabilities out there, using progressive enhancement in your applications means they can have much wider reach. In the long run, it also means less work—progressive enhancement makes your application both backward compatible and future-proof.

Here are the core principles of progressive enhancement:

- Basic content should be accessible to all browsers
- Basic functionality should be accessible to all browsers
- Sparse, semantic markup contains all content
- Enhanced layout is provided by externally linked CSS
- Enhanced behavior is provided by unobtrusive, externally linked JavaScript
- End-user browser preferences are respected

—Wikipedia, "Progressive Enhancement" (retrieved September 2, 2008)

Keep in mind that not all scripting events need to be made keyboard-accessible; it is the *function* that needs to be. We're not trying to make the keyboard act like the mouse, we're trying to make the keyboard a first-class input mechanism.

Disappearing (and Reappearing) Acts

One of the most common accessibility issues is showing and hiding content: pop-up menus, expanding/collapsing outlines, and rollovers (to name a few). We discuss these issues with some of the most common techniques used to solve them, and then look at an example in depth to show what makes it work and why we want it to work this way.

Our primary goals are keyboard activation and appropriate reading order.

Keyboard activation

Your first task is to make the basic content and functionality of your menu accessible to all browsers by using sparse, semantic markup:

- Mark menu items as links
- Organize links in nested lists
- Create subpages that mirror the pop-up submenu pages

After creating a solid foundation, manage the layout with externally linked CSS. Finally, enhance the behavior of your site with unobtrusive, externally linked JavaScript. Here are some things to watch out for when you use CSS and scripting.

Issues with :hover

There are many beautiful examples that use :hover to create a CSS-only pop-up menu, in which the code is elegant and works well across browsers and platforms. The problem is that the :hover pseudoselector in CSS is only activated by mouse movements and is usually associated with an inactive element, such as a heading or list item. In this section, we focus on the issues with :hover on active elements, and in the next section, we discuss issues with using :hover with inactive elements.

The following example uses :hover to display a submenu:

```
/* css */
#nav ul li:hover ul
  {
    display:block; position:absolute; top:0;
    left:164px;  border: 1px solid #6C4571
  }
...
/* html */
<div id="nav">
<ul>
    <li><a href="first.html" class="first">one</a>
        <ul>
            <li><a href="sub-two.html">sub-one</a></li>
            <li><a href="sub-three.html">sub-two</a></li>
        </ul>
    </li>
...
```

This works great for someone using a mouse, but to make this accessible by a keyboard or touchscreen, your first inclination may be to look to the :focus pseudoselector. Unfortunately, :focus is only active while the current element has focus. In the example just shown, when the parent (menu item) loses focus, the children (submenu items) disappear.

You also need to consider how the children are hidden: using display:none or positioning them offscreen. If you use display:none, there is no way to tab to the children—they never receive focus and are never displayed. If you position them offscreen, you can tab to them, but they won't be displayed. Because

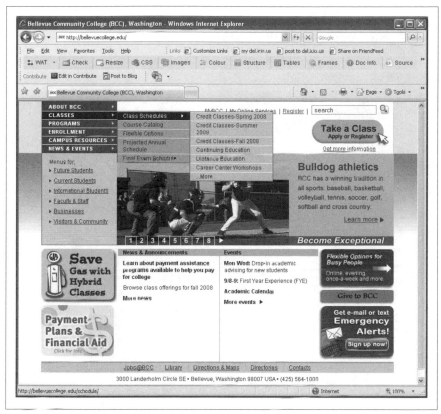

Figure 8-1. Screenshot of Bellevue Community College home page with nested menus open

positioning the ul offscreen hides the children and because the ul can't take focus, there is no way to override the positioning properties of each element. When links are hidden offscreen, a person must tab to every link in the menu; there is no way to skip between menu items.

> The keyboard support for visibility:hidden and display:none is the same. The difference between the two is that with visibility:hidden browsers reserve space for the elements, whereas with display:none space is not created until the element is made visible.

The Bellevue Community College home page organizes links into nested lists and relies on the :hover pseudoselector to position and show/hide submenus. Figure 8-1 shows the BCC home page submenus of "Classes," which users open by hovering over "Classes" and "Class Schedules" with the mouse.

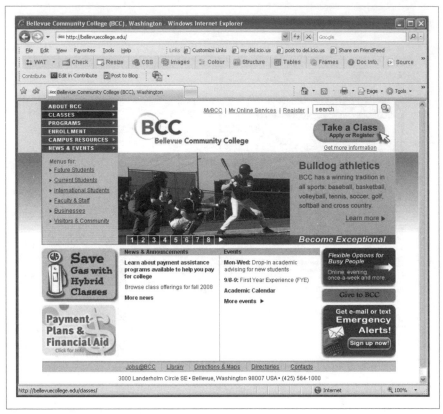

Figure 8-2. BCC home page, "Classes" has focus

When tabbing through the BCC site, you will only know that you have reached one of the submenu items by reading the status bar of the browser. Figure 8-2 shows the BCC home page with the keyboard focus on the "Classes" menu item.

Pressing the Tab key once more moves focus to the first submenu item of "Classes," but it is displayed offscreen. A screen reader doesn't care that it is offscreen and will read and interact with the menu as though it were in the viewport. However, for someone using a keyboard because of a physical disability, the only way to know that the submenu has focus is to look at the status bar. See Figure 8-3.

Figure 8-3. "Schedule" has focus but is not visible

Because the BCC site is designed with accessibility in mind, if you press Enter while "About BCC" has keyboard focus, it activates the link to the About BCC page that lists all of the submenu items on that page, shown in Figure 8-4.

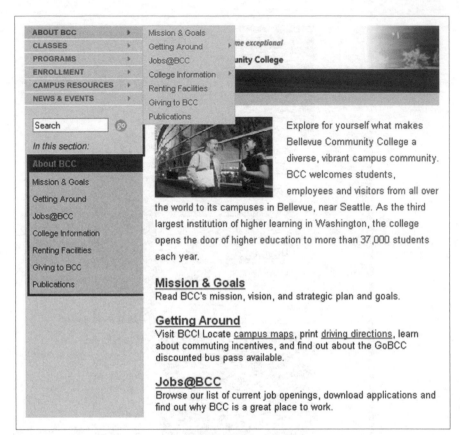

Figure 8-4. About BCC page lists links to the submenu items: Mission & Goals, Getting Around, Jobs@BCC, etc.

Therefore, this is technically accessible. However, navigating to the "Classes" link requires pressing the Tab key 20 times. Figure 8-5 shows the nesting of the submenu items and the number of links between the "About BCC" and "Classes" submenus.

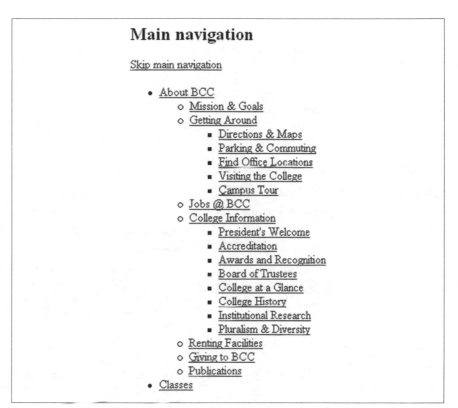

Figure 8-5. BCC home page without style sheets shows the nested list structure of the page

We could leave this as it is, as it's technically accessible to people who are not using a mouse—whether they are using a screen reader, using the keyboard only (e.g., a mobile device), or using a touchscreen (e.g., an iPhone).

But, what if you wanted to make it *more* accessible? There are several paths to travel, and none is perfect today:

- Use `:focus` and `:active` to make the submenus visible as you tab through them.
- Use `display:none` to hide the submenus, and use the top-level menu items to link to subpages with links.
- Use `onclick()` to show and hide submenus.

BCC is working toward a more accessible solution and should have something in place soon after the publication of this book.

With all of these options, we are interacting with the menus as links rather than simply as menus. Table 8-1 summarizes the differences between expected behaviors of interacting with links and system menus via the keyboard.

Table 8-1. Keypresses and their outcomes, with links versus system menus

Key press	Expected behavior with a link	Expected behavior with a system menu
Tab	Move to next link on the page	Windows XP: error. Focus does not move. Mac OS X: move focus to next top-level menu.
Right arrow	Web browser: none Assistive technology: read the link text character by character or move to the next link	When the menu bar or a menu item has focus, pressing the right arrow causes focus to move to the next menu, or if the current menu item has a submenu, it will open the submenu.
Escape	None	Close the open menu or submenu (Windows then returns focus to the parent menu item, while in Mac OS X the focus returns to the application window).
Enter	Activate the link	If the menu item has a submenu, open the submenu; otherwise, activate the current menu item.

Typical keyboard behaviors for widgets are being debated and documented in the DHTML Style Guide (*http://dev.aol.com/ dhtml_style_guide*). Many of the same people working on this guide are also working on ARIA, and the two documents have been feeding off of one another for some time.

Building a menu out of links puts us somewhere between links and system menus. Using the BCC site as an example, we could add an onclick event to each link so that instead of activating the link and opening a new page, it could display the submenu item. Pressing Tab again could take us to the first submenu item. But, what do we do about other keystrokes? Do we trap arrow keys and the Escape key and replicate system behavior? We tried this out and had a few people test it. They found it confusing.

Many people recommend the "Ultimate Drop Down Menu 4" by James Edwards (*http://www.udm4.com/*). There are a number of things we like about UDM4. First and foremost, it's one of the cleanest implementations of a dropdown menu that we've encountered. It uses standard XHTML and separates its CSS and JavaScript into external files. It's extremely customizable. And its menu markup uses HTML headings, which allow screen readers to navigate with their own built-in headings mode. Among the commercial menu products out there, we think it's one of the best.

That's not to say it's perfect. When we tested it with versions of the JAWS and NVDA screen readers, we found some anomalies that prevent it from being used like a system menu (although the screen readers themselves share some responsibility for this, and we had more trouble with nearly every other menu script out there).

And the licensing terms may not appeal to many people. While it can be used at no charge on noncommercial sites, those users are required by license to link to UDM4's site on every page with a UDM4 menu. Commercial licenses are available on various terms, either for a one-time or subscription fee, but they also contain restrictions that you should read before purchasing the product.

If you can live with UDM4's licensing regime, it's a good product and can save you a lot of time. But we've known many folks who can't agree to its terms for one reason or another, and we think it's important to show how to achieve our universal design goals in a menu system, without the licensing restrictions. So we wrote an open source menu script of our own, which you can download at *http://ud4wa.com*.

So, where are we today?

- Limit the number of menu items.
- Provide subpages that link to all of the submenu items.
- Test with intended audience to determine what kind of behavior they expect.

When the item to activate isn't an active element

Pseudoselectors such as `:focus` and `:active` work only on active elements such as links and input elements, and they do not work in Microsoft's Internet Explorer (version 7 and earlier). Those using a screen reader can navigate to inactive elements (such as headings and list items) so that they may be read aloud. But this doesn't activate `:focus` because the screen reader is not moving the browser focus but instead is moving its own virtual cursor and therefore its own virtual focus.

In Figure 8-6, the course names are marked as labels.

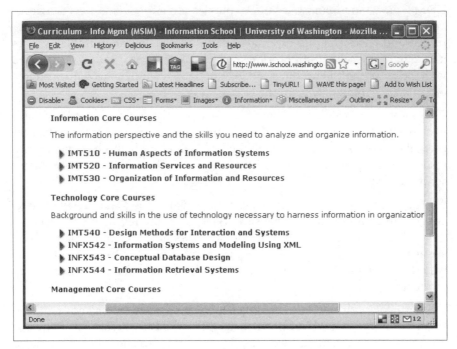

Figure 8-6. List of course descriptions—collapsed

Clicking on a course name expands to show a course description, as shown in Figure 8-7.

The markup is very elegant. We particularly like using `label` to label a `div`:

```
<label style="cursor: pointer;" class="collapsible"
for="section6"><img src="courses.aspx_files/closed.jpg" alt="
[expand] ">IMT530 –
Organization of Information and Resources</label>
<div style="display: none;" class="collapsed" id="section6">
<p class="content">Introduction to issues in organization of
information and information objects including:
analysis of intellectual
and physical characteristics of information objects; use of metadata
and metadata standards for information systems; theory of
classification, including semantic relationships and facet analysis;
creation of controlled vocabularies; and display and arrangement. </p>
</div>
```

The problem for keyboard users is that label elements cannot receive focus, even though the HTML spec says they should.

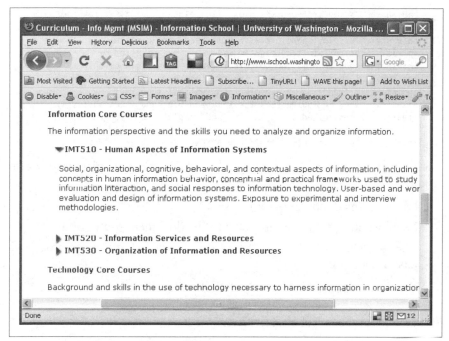

Figure 8-7. List of course descriptions—expanded

One aspect of ARIA that we cover here is `tabindex`. According to the HTML 4.01 specification, `tabindex` applies only to the `A`, `AREA`, `BUTTON`, `INPUT`, `OBJECT`, `SELECT`, and `TEXTAREA` elements (*http://www.w3.org/TR/REC-html40/interact/forms.html#adef-tabindex*). `tabindex` values can be any number between 0 and 32,767 and are navigated according to the following rules:

- Elements with a positive `tabindex` value are navigated in order of lowest `tabindex` value to highest. Elements with the same `tabindex` value are navigated in document source order.

- Elements without a `tabindex` attribute or with a `tabindex` of "0" are navigated next and in the order they appear in the document source.

- Disabled elements are not included in the tab order.

ARIA slightly changes the rules by allowing any visible element to be added to the tab order. ARIA also adds a negative value for `tabindex`. An element with a negative `tabindex` is not added to the tab order, but it can receive focus via the mouse or JavaScript `element.focus()`. This allows an application to support arrow key navigation—as we'll see in the next chapter.

```
<div tabindex="-1">...</div>
<p><a href="example1.html">Example link 1</a></p>
<label style="cursor: pointer;" class="collapsible" for="section6"
```

```
tabindex="0"><img src="courses.aspx_files/closed.jpg" alt=" [expand]
">IMT530 - Organization of Information and Resources</label>
<div style="display: none;" class="collapsed" id="section6">
<p class="content">Introduction to issues in organization of
information and information objects including: analysis of intellectual
and physical characteristics of information objects; use of metadata
and metadata standards for information systems; theory of
classification, including semantic relationships and facet analysis;
creation of controlled vocabularies; and display and arrangement. </p>
</div>
<p><a href="example2.html" tabindex="1">Example link 2</a></p>
```

According to the ARIA-enhanced tabindex scheme, the tab order for this code would be as follows:

- Example link 2—because `tabindex="1"`
- Example link 1—because it is next in the document source order
- The IMT530 label—because it is next in the document source order and has `tabindex="0"`

The div with `tabindex="-1"` is not included in the tab order.

When you don't need an equivalent for :hover

Using `:hover` to highlight items that can not receive focus (such as lines in a table) is cool—it helps people who are visual learners. The person using a screen reader will know which item has focus—as only one item at a time can have focus. For example, in the following code, the current row is highlighted on `:hover`:

```
<style type="text/css">

  tr:hover {background-color: #FFCC33;}
</style>
```

Note that we're doing this with a style sheet rather than a scripted `onmouseover()`. When possible, we prefer using CSS to scripting.

Issues with device-specific events

Catching mouse events with `onmouseover` has similar issues to `:hover`—it may work for someone using a mouse but not for keyboard or mobile users. Even modern mobile devices such as the iPhone have trouble with `onmouseover`, since they track only users tapping on the screen.

There's no reason not to use `onmouseover` per se. However, if you do use it for anything more complex than to call out the presence of a link (say, to show or hide tiles in a trivia game), you will need to use another event as well, for example, `onfocus`, `onactivate`, `onkeypress`, or even `onclick`.

For more information, WebAIM's Creating Accessible JavaScript: JavaScript Event Handlers provides a great overview (*http://www.webaim.org/techniques/javascript/eventhandlers.php*).

Summary

Using Unobtrusive JavaScript, we are able to add interesting functionality to any web page and make it accessible to people using a variety of devices.

Ajax and WAI-ARIA

In the last chapter, we showed you how to add JavaScript to your HTML and CSS to make a web application. In this chapter, we discuss adding Accessible Rich Internet Application (WAI-ARIA, or ARIA for short) properties and other techniques for making JavaScript and Ajax accessible.

We have yet to realize the non-disability-specific benefits of ARIA, although we expect to see the mobile market take advantage of many of the ARIA features. For example, drag-and-drop is something that is not widely supported across mobile devices, even on the iPhone (as of late 2008).

A report from Informa Telecoms & Media (2007) predicts that 50% of the world's population will have access to the Internet via a mobile device by 2010. Many of these devices will not support scripting or embedded objects. The majority of currently available mobile devices have a screen resolution of 240x320 pixels, and the iPhone isn't much bigger at 480x320. Therefore, with smaller screen sizes, rich applications designed for desktop environments are not likely to fit entirely on the screen.

These similarities—constraints on viewport size and lack of a mouse—should cause mobile developers to take a look at WAI-ARIA and other accessibility APIs. The techniques you are looking for may already exist.

Taking Stock of Existing Code

Designing web applications without Ajax, while more complicated than our earlier exercises with simple HTML, is still pretty straightforward. In addition to what you've learned about images, forms, tables, frames, and the like, you will need to take a look at how your site is implemented at the server level, as well as how you are using script to make your users' lives easier.

Once you've taken stock of all the script and server magic you use to glue your site together, separate it into three categories: code that works well universally, code that can be made to work universally, and code that needs to be a workaround.

Code That Works Well Universally

You may look at a script-based feature in your site and find no problems with it either in mobile devices or assistive technology. In some cases, the site may even function better than it would otherwise; for example, it may take fewer keystrokes to enter data. Not only is this the best outcome, it's what we hope you've learned to do with all your code after reading this book. Part of universal design is building intelligence into software components so that they can be reused again and again. Why redo work you've already done?

Code That Can Be Made to Work Universally

Let's say that you evaluate your web application, and it doesn't work on a class of mobile devices. Is it a limitation of the technology, or could it in fact be modified or rewritten to work elsewhere? This is your chance to build a better toolkit: where the need and the ability meet.

Code That Needs a Workaround

Sometimes, there is no easy way to make a component work everywhere, particularly with assistive technology. It could be that this code is too brittle to be modified, or it's part of a library that you can't change, or you simply don't have time to rewrite it properly.

In these cases, it's important that the key function of that code is available some other way, be it through a server transaction or through what we call graceful degradation. (This is the flip side of progressive enhancement, which we discuss later.)

Support in Browsers

On the desktop, Ajax is now old hat. All major browsers have full support for `XmlHttpRequest`, the core object of Ajax, which fetches data and allows a developer to insert new information into a document without a page refresh. Until recently (the dawn of the iPhone era), device-based browsing has lacked support. With a limited ability to interact with Ajax controls, it is imperative to practice progressive enhancement.

Moreover, people authoring Ajax-based controls must understand that even with Ajax support in web-enabled devices, mouse interaction may be extremely limited. For example, how do you execute a `mouseover` with a touchscreen, which registers only taps? The Nokia N800 series is an excellent example. Although, it does have a Mozilla-based browser and Flash 9, `mouseover` events are totally unreliable on the device.

Support in Assistive Technology

How has Ajax been supported in assistive technology? Not well. Remember that while JavaScript is in some ways supported by assistive technology, it's still reading HTML as a format for more or less static documents. Further complicating matters is how Ajax came to be—through Microsoft's introduction of an ActiveX control called XMLHTTP. (The `XmlHttpRequest` object has since been submitted to the W3C for formal standardization.)

Today's assistive technology can't deal well with asynchronous data being inserted, and so nearly all Ajax-based content comes with accessibility problems. As a result, the accessibility techniques traditionally associated with Ajax have been in the vein of progressive enhancement. In other words, the techniques provide users a way to opt out of the rich experience. Jeremy Keith coined the term "Hijax" to describe this approach.

If people had imagined when `XmlHttpRequest` was created that a brew of HTML, script, and asynchronous XML data would become a leading method for creating web user interfaces, they did a great job keeping the rest of us in the dark. Assistive technology depends on an understanding of the semantics of any given object you see on the screen: specifically, an object's name and description, but also its *role* and *state*.

Role and state can be most easily described as what a control does and its current configuration. In HTML, the roles and states for links and form controls are well defined, and we rely almost solely on this information for the purposes of accessibility. For example, the *checkbox* role has states of checked and unchecked. We take this kind of contract between the language and its behavior for granted when it comes to working well with assistive technology.

But what if I want to create a slider control? HTML doesn't define a control and (before ARIA) we were not able to assign roles and states to controls we created using HTML alone.

Direct Accessibility—WAI-ARIA

ARIA is the fastest-moving advance in web accessibility. It's supported in all major browsers: IE 8, Mozilla 3, Opera 9.5, and Safari 4. Frameworks including Dojo, Google Web Toolkit, and the Yahoo! User Interface Library have built-in support, and the makers of the JAWS and Window-Eyes screen readers have implemented ARIA as well. It doesn't stop there. Communities are building support in open source assistive technologies, such as Orca and NVDA. Google implemented AxsJAX, scripts that inject web pages with ARIA properties. Charles Chen, who authored AxsJAX, also created Fire Vox, an add-on to Firefox that makes it a self-voicing browser. This vocabulary is the key to unlocking Ajax accessibility.

> That said, ARIA has not reached W3C Recommendations status, which means the current specification could (and likely will) change; and while many browsers and assistive technologies have begun implementing ARIA, these implementations are not complete and not all users have these new versions.
>
> Since this is a new area, we have not addressed all of the important and revolutionary concepts introduced with ARIA. For the latest information, refer to the WAI-ARIA Overview (*http://www.w3.org/WAI/intro/aria*) and the Code Talks wiki (*http://wiki.codetalks.org*).

Before delving into examples of how to implement ARIA, it's important to know exactly what makes it necessary. ARIA functions as a bridge between web and software accessibility. All of this information—role and state, live regions, focus management—corresponds to the typical information required in a software application.

Most of this is well covered in HTML. Every form field in HTML 4.01, for example, has a role in Microsoft Active Accessibility (MSAA) that clearly corresponds. It's the new controls introduced by the scripting frameworks that make ARIA useful. Let's say someone has developed a combo box by grafting a text field onto a select box. Or maybe he created the entire control out of an empty div and some DOM scripting. The way to turn that blob of HTML into something semantically useful again is to define its roles and states in ARIA. To put it another way, ARIA exists so that you can express semantics that can't be expressed in HTML alone.

Process/mindset

> Plan for Ajax from the start. Implement Ajax at the end.[*]
>
> —Jeremy Keith

The progression for designing Ajax applications is to make the page work at each of these stages with each of these technologies:

1. HTML—the basic structure of the application
2. CSS—layout and style
3. Server-side scripts (PHP, Python, ASP, Ruby on Rails, etc.)—adding or changing content on HTTP requests and page refresh
4. Ajax—getting rid of page refresh to add and change content (using Hijax as necessary, ensuring keyboard access to all functionality)
5. ARIA—set roles on unidentifiable objects, create programmatically determinable relationships, and keep states and properties up-to-date

In *Bulletproof Ajax* (New Riders), Jeremy Keith writes:

> Before Ajax, a Web site worked like a self-service restaurant. Every time you wanted some information, the browser had to fetch a new page. In a self-service restaurant, whenever you want some food, you have to go up to the counter to order it.
>
> Adding Ajax to a Web site is like hiring a waiter for a restaurant. The customer no longer needs to go to the counter to order food. The waiter will take the order to the counter instead. This results in a much more pleasant dining experience.
>
> Just because you've hired a waiter doesn't mean you can fire the cook. Yet this is exactly what some Ajax applications attempt to do. Not content with having a waiter take orders and bring food, they get the waiter to do all the cooking too.
>
> Cooking should happen in the kitchen. Application logic belongs on the server. It's better for everyone that way. Your application will work more consistently when it is server-based. The browser environment is simply too unpredictable.

This unpredictability will only increase as your audience accesses your site from more devices, in more situations, and with a growing range of personal preferences. Whether it be due to security reasons or device capabilities, you cannot assume everyone in your worldwide audience will experience Ajax. Layering the experience in a single application so that the environment can transform to meet everyone's needs. Creating a single flexible application decreases your maintenance costs because all of the various end-user experiences run off of the same code on the server. Keep in mind that a "single flexible application" does not mean making your site work with a single style sheet or

---

[*] *http://domscripting.com/presentations/wd06/hijax/*

set of scripts. Once your application has a solid HTML foundation and the bulk of the functionality is on the server, you can tack on as many CSS and client-side scriptable building blocks as you like. See Chapter 4 for more on creating CSS for different devices.

Roles

In HTML, most of the elements have a defined role and behavior: an a is a link, h1 is a first-level heading, and so on. However, because HTML was primarily designed as a document markup language, there are many objects that HTML does not define. Examples include div and span, which can be used to do any number of things from grouping elements into a section to creating a button. As such, assistive technologies don't know what to make of them. ARIA provides over 50 roles to choose from, as shown in Table 9-1.

Table 9-1. WAI-ARIA roles[a]

alert	directory	main	radio	tab
alertdialog	document	marquee	radiogroup	tablist
application	grid	menu	region	tabpanel
banner	gridcell	menubar	row	textbox
button	group	menuitem	rowheader	timer
checkbox	heading	menuitemcheckbox	search	toolbar
columnheader	img	menuitemradio	secondary	tooltip
combobox	link	navigation	seealso	tree
contentinfo	list	note	separator	treegrid
definition	listbox	option	slider	treeitem
description	listitem	presentation	spinbutton	
dialog	log	progressbar	status	

[a] *http://www.w3.org/TR/wai-aria/#roles*—February 4, 2008 Working Draft

In the previous chapter, we showed a menu with submenus. Marking the parent ul as a menubar and each list item as a menu item will let the user agent map the role to one of the objects in the OS-level accessibility API. Roles can be used like classes in that a single object can have multiple roles, and as with classes you use a space-separated list. In the case of our menu, it is a structural item and needs only one role:

```
<ul role="menubar">
  <li role="menuitem"><a href="http://bellevuecollege.edu/about/"
class="first" id="first">About BCC</a>
    <ul role="menu">
      <li role="menuitem"><a
```

```
    href="http://bellevuecollege.edu/about/goals/">Mission &amp;
Goals</a></li>
        <li role="menuitem"><a
  href="http://bellevuecollege.edu/about/around/">Getting Around</a></li>
  ...
  </ul>
```

States and properties

As with HTML elements, after you have chosen one, you can tweak it with a
variety of attributes. With ARIA roles, we have several properties to choose
from. In the case of the menubar, the following are the available properties:

- `activedescendant`
- `atomic`
- `busy`
- `channel`
- `controls`
- `expanded`
- `live`
- `relevant`
- `templateid`

The global states are also available:

- `datatype`
- `describedby`
- `dropeffect`
- `flowto`
- `grab`
- `haspopup`
- `hidden`
- `labelledby`
- `owns`

 ARIA properties must be prefixed with `aria-` as in
`aria-haspopup`—as you will see in our code examples. There
is one exception: role does *not* need the `aria` prefix. When
discussing ARIA properties in text (as in the previous para-
graph), we will refer to properties without the prefix.

In the following example, we initially want the menu to be collapsed (`aria-expanded="false"`) and want it to appear in the tab order (`tabindex="0"`, although because we're using links, they will appear in the tab order as active HTML elements). The `aria-haspopup` property causes a screen reader to notify a person that submenu items exist:

```
<ul role="menubar">
  <li role="menuitem" aria-haspopup="true" aria-expanded="false"
tabindex="0"><a href="http://bellevuecollege.edu/about/" class="first"
id="first">About BCC</a>
      <ul role="menu">
          <li role="menuitem"><a
href="http://bellevuecollege.edu/about/goals/">Mission &amp;
Goals</a></li>
          <li role="menuitem"><a href="http://bellevuecollege.edu
/about/around/">Getting Around</a></li>
      ...
  </ul>
```

Handling navigation and keyboard support

In the last chapter, we started handling keyboard support, but one thing was missing. It is very difficult to track and change focus in today's browsers using only HTML and scripting. Here's another venue where ARIA can shine.

Since a mouse has only a few events that it can fire, it's not surprising that mouse events are well handled and standardized: when you hover over an object more information about it might pop up, or when you click on an object it does something. Keyboard conventions aren't so well developed. A standard keyboard typically has 101 keys (give or take a few) that can be pressed 1 or 2 or 3 at a time. Mac keyboards differ from Windows keyboards differ from Linux keyboards; English keyboards differ from French keyboards differ from Japanese keyboards. I've lost track of how many possible keyboard combinations that is....

There are several commonly used practices on Windows—Alt+F typically opens an application's File menubar. Pressing the Enter key activates selected items, like submitting a form. The Escape key usually allows you to back out of an operation. Arrow keys are used to navigate menus.

However, there are OS-specific keyboard commands, browser-specific keyboard commands, as well as assistive technology-specific. Add on top of those application-specific keyboard commands, and managing keyboard collisions has become an art form in the assistive technology world—and is one of the requirements of Section 508.

Unfortunately for Ajax, it is a relatively new concept. If you define a new component, you will have to define its keyboard support. WAI-ARIA Best Practices describes `optionKeyEvent`—a function to handle keystrokes for a widget—at *http://www.w3.org/TR/2008/WD-wai-aria-practices-20080204/#accessible widget.*

Luckily, there are lots of folks writing scripts to handle this behavior, which can be borrowed, or they are building it into widgets in the toolkits. Example 9-1 shows some of the keyboard support from the Mozilla bare-bones "spreadsheet" example (*http://www.mozilla.org/access/dhtml/spreadsheet*).

Example 9-1. JavaScript for connecting keyboard commands to widgets

```
Menubar.prototype.doNavigation = function(event) {
  var bEventContinue = true;  // browser can still use event
  var key = event.keyCode;
  if ((key >=KEY_LEFT && key <= KEY_DOWN) || key == KEY_ESCAPE) {
    var idx = this.getActiveMenuIndex();
    if (idx < 0) {
      idx = 0;
    }
    // if subIndex > -1 a submenu is open - up and down movement will
occur in it
    var subIndex = this.getActiveSubIndex();
    var subMenuId = this.getActiveSubOpen();
    var menus = this.getMenus();
    var menuLen = menus.length;
    var activeMenuId = menus[idx];
    var curDrop = document.getElementById(activeMenuId + DROP_SUFFIX);

    if (key == KEY_LEFT || key == KEY_RIGHT) {

      var nextIdx = idx;
      if (key == KEY_LEFT) { // left
        nextIdx = (idx + (menuLen-1)) % menuLen;
      }
      else { // right
        nextIdx = ((idx + 1) % menuLen);
      }
      // if drop menu is displayed, close it and open the next one
or move into submenu
      var bShowNext = this.isActiveOpen();
      if (bShowNext) {
        // current drop is open, see if it has submenu
        if (curDrop) {
          if (subMenuId != null) {
            // submenu is open - close it
            this.hideSubMenu();
            if (key == KEY_LEFT) {
              // find parentItem and set focus to it
              gFocusItem = document.getElementById(subMenuId);
              setTimeout("doFocus();",0);
              return false;
            }
            // if right just close and move to next top level menu
```

```
(which happens below)
            } // end of submenu open
            if (key == KEY_RIGHT && subMenuId == null) {
                // if right arrow and submenu are not open, get current item
in the drop-down and see if it has a submenu
                var itemIdx = this.getActiveItemIndex();
                var menuItems = this.getMenuItems(activeMenuId);
                var curItemInDrop= document.getElementById(menuItems[itemIdx]);
                var bHasSubMenu = this.hasSubMenu(curItemInDrop);
                if (bHasSubMenu == true) {
                    return this.showSubMenu(event,curItemInDrop.getAttribute
("id"));

                }
            }
            // if haven't returned yet - then close the current drop
            curDrop.style.display = "none"; // only one menudrop child per menu
            this.setActiveItemIndex(0);
        }
    }
    this.setActiveMenuIndex(nextIdx);
    var nextMenuId = menus[nextIdx];
    gFocusItem=document.getElementById(nextMenuId + TOP_SUFFIX);
    if (bShowNext == true) {
      var drop = document.getElementById(nextMenuId + DROP_SUFFIX);
      if (drop) {
        drop.style.display="block";
        var menuItems = this.getMenuItems(nextMenuId);
        gFocusItem=document.getElementById(menuItems[0]);
      }
    }
    setTimeout("doFocus();",0);
  }

  if (key == KEY_UP || key == KEY_DOWN ) {
    var itemIdx = this.getActiveItemIndex();
    var bOpen = this.isActiveOpen();

    if (curDrop) {
      // first see if submenu is open
      if (subMenuId != null) {
        // submenu is open - move within it
        var subMenus = this.getSubMenuItems(subMenuId);
        var subLen = subMenus.length;
        var nextSubIndex =subIndex;
        if (key == KEY_DOWN) {
          nextSubIndex = (subIndex +1) % subLen;
        }
        else if (key == KEY_UP) {
          nextSubIndex = (subIndex + (subLen - 1)) % subLen;
        }
        gFocusItem = document.getElementById(subMenus[nextSubIndex]);
        this.setActiveSubIndex(nextSubIndex);
        setTimeout("doFocus();",0);
```

```
        return false;

      } // end of if submenus - back to regular processing

      var menuItems = this.getMenuItems(activeMenuId);
      var itemLen = menuItems.length;
      var nextItemIdx;
      if (!bOpen) { // open and set to the first item
        this.showMenu(event, activeMenuId, true);
        itemIdx = -1;
      }
      if (itemIdx == -1) {
        nextItemIdx = 0;
      }
      else if (key == KEY_DOWN ){
        nextItemIdx = (itemIdx +1) % itemLen;
      }
      else { //UP
        nextItemIdx = (itemIdx + (itemLen-1)) % itemLen;
      }

      this.setActiveItemIndex(nextItemIdx);
      gFocusItem=document.getElementById(menuItems[nextItemIdx]);
      setTimeout("doFocus();",0);
    } // end of id curDrop
  } // end of id up/down
// need to prevent propagation of arrow keys
/*  try {
     ev.preventDefault();
   }
  catch (err) {
    try {
      ev.returnValue=false;
    }
    catch (errNext) {
      ;
    }
  }
}*/
bEventContinue = false;

if (key == KEY_ESCAPE ) {
    this.closeMenu(event);
    bEventContinue = false;
    if (gFocusBeforeMenus) {
      gFocusItem  = gFocusBeforeMenus;
      setTimeout("doFocus();",0);
    }
    else {
      document.focus();
    }
  } // end of if KEY_ESCAPE
  } // end of if arrow or escape  key
  return bEventContinue;
}
```

Managing focus

Part of making your keyboard handlers work properly is managing focus changes as a user interacts with your application. Sometimes you will need to move focus to a particular element, whereas other times you will be watching for focus changes. For complex widgets, such as a tree structure, you'll want the parent to be in the tab order, but all of the children don't have to be. In this case, put a `tabindex` on the container element and use `activedescendant` to change the focus between children. See the following resources to learn more:

- WAI-ARIA Best Practices, Section 3.2 Providing Keyboard Focus (*http:// www.w3.org/WAI/PF/aria-practices/#kbd_focus*)
- Keyboard-navigable JS widgets (*http://wiki.codetalks.org/wiki/index.php/ Docs/Keyboard_navigable_JS_widgets*)

Dealing with updates

In their article "Making Ajax Work with Screen Readers" (*http://juicystudio .com/article/making-ajax-work-with-screen-readers.php*), Gez Lemon and Steve Faulkner describe how screen readers use a virtual buffer to interact with elements displayed onscreen. The virtual buffer is usually only updated on page refresh or when the user changes modes. As screen readers get better at handling updates, one of the features in ARIA is the ability to tell a component when and how to present the user with updates as they happen.

ARIA defines four priority settings:

off
> Do not update the user.

polite
> Update the user when he is not busy.

assertive
> Update the user as soon as possible, but do not interrupt the user.

rude
> Update the user immediately, interrupting everything, including the last rude update.

For example, as you edit a tweet in Twitter, the number of characters left is updated as you type. If you are sighted, how often do you glance at that number? Probably only when you pause to edit your tweet. Therefore, in this example you would use `aria-live="polite"` so that when you pause, your assistive technology can update you.

On the other hand, if you were about to send an email to everyone in your address book, you would want an alert to interrupt you as soon as it detected the possibility. Be careful with the assertive and rude roles, though. It may seem like a good idea to have your clock widget reading out every second, but after about half a minute of listening to the screen reader chattering, you will quickly realize the error of your ways. Most of the time in ARIA, as in life, polite is the way to go.

Building on the bare-bones spreadsheet, we can add a function to sort the columns when selected. Using Stuart Langridge's sorttable script (as described at *http://woork.blogspot.com/2008/02/sort-table-rows-using-ajax.html*), we need to make the spreadsheet a live region. We make it "assertive," as we don't need to interrupt the user, but we do want to notify her that the sort is finished. (We also add `class="sortable"` to use Stuart's script.)

```
<table tabindex="0"  id="table2" class="sortable" role="grid"
aria-live="assertive" aria-activedescendant="row1col1" >
```

Using Unobtrusive JavaScript, attach onkeydown and onfocus event handlers to the table.

If a component controls another part of the web page or application, explicitly identify this relationship using `aria-controls`. For someone with sight, you will likely have created visual cues to alert them to changes in content. Using the `aria-controls` attribute will allow a person using an assistive technology to follow the same path and find the updated content.

aria-flowto

The `flowto` attribute is a more elegant approach to setting reading order in an application. Instead of setting a numeric `tabindex` value (which can become a serious pain when the numbers are too close to one another), this attribute allows you to point directly to the next control in the reading order. And unlike `tabindex`, it's possible to have multiple controls pointing to the same item (say, the subtotal in a shopping cart), which is perfect for marking up a flowchart, as shown in Figure 9-1.

Assume we use CSS to position the images, using this HTML:

```
<img src="start.png" id="start" alt="start"
flowto="question-90" />
<img src="90-question.png" id="question-90" alt="The 90's?"
flowto="no yes" />
<img src="no.png" id="no" alt="no" flowto="stop1" />
<img src="yes.png" id="yes" alt="yes" flowto="stop2" />
<img src="stop.png" id="stop1" alt="stop"/>
<img src="stop.png" id="stop2" alt="stop" flowto="hammertime
collaborate" />
<img src="hammertime.png" id="hammertime" alt="hammertime"/>
```

```
<img src="collaborate.png" id="collaborate" alt="collaborate"
flowto="listen" />
<img src="listen.png" id="listen" alt="listen"/>
```

While this is a fun example, it would be more relevant to look at a spreadsheet and specify a reading order through the cells to guide someone through an interpretation of the data. Also note that as of this writing, no screen reader supports this attribute.

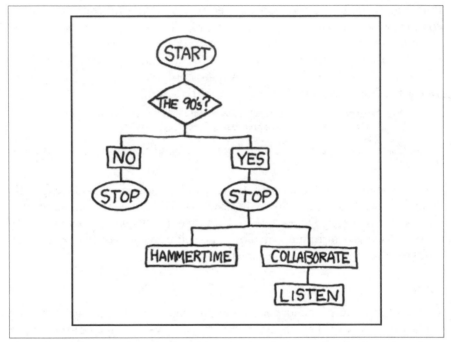

Figure 9-1. "Freestyle rapping is basically applied Markov chains" (Source: http://xkcd.com/ 210/)

aria-labelledby and aria-describedby

Another feature in ARIA is the ability to point from a control to its label and description. We know about the `label` element discussed in Chapter 5: it defines a label, and binds it to a control. The `aria-labelledby` attribute is the inverse of that: it assigns the control to the ID of a label elsewhere in the document. The `aria-describedby` attribute lets you assign a description to a given control as well.

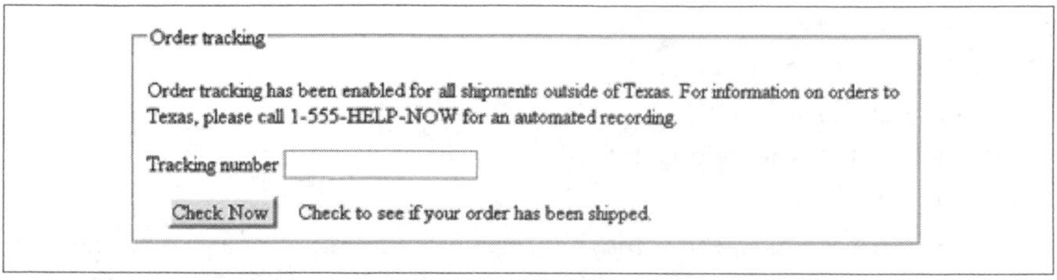

Figure 9-2. Screenshot of http://www.mozilla.org/access/dhtml/button

Figure 9-2 shows the form created by the following code. When someone using a screen reader enters the form, the first description (`groupdesc1`) should be read. When the focus moves to the Check Now button, its description (`buttondesc1`) should be read, giving the person additional information about the button.

```
<fieldset aria-describedby="groupdesc1">
  <legend>Order tracking</legend>
  <div role="description" id="groupdesc1">
    Order tracking has been enabled for all shipments outside of Texas.
For
    information on orders to Texas, please call 1-555-HELP-NOW for an
automated
    recording.
  </div>

  <div>
    <label for="tracknum">Tracking number</label>
    <input id="tracknum" type="text"/>
  </div>

  <div>
    <span role="button"  tabindex="0" aria-describedby="buttondesc1" >
    Check Now
    </span>
    <p role="description" id="buttondesc1">
      Check to see if your order has been shipped.
    </p>
  </div>
</fieldset>
```

Using Unobtrusive JavaScript, attach `onkeydown` and `onclick` event handlers to the button.

Error handling, part 2

Chapter 5's discussion of error handling outlines a few issues to watch out for when making forms accessible, including identifying required fields, alerting the user to input errors, and indicating which fields contain errors. WAI-ARIA contains two properties and HTML has one role to address these issues:

`aria-required="true"`
> Indicates that a field is required.

`aria-invalid="true"`
> Indicates that the field is not valid.

`role="alert"`
> Indicates that a section is playing the role of an alert. There is some Java-Script trickery required to make this appear as an alert (adding it to the DOM with the role of `alert` should cause a browser to fire an alert event to an assistive technology).

Marco Zehe's blog "Easy ARIA tip #3: aria-invalid and role 'alert'" ties all of these concepts together in a tutorial with working examples (*http://www.mar cozehe.de/2008/07/16/easy-aria-tip-3-aria-invalid-and-role-alert/*).

Disabling controls

Before ARIA, if a control, such as a "previous page" button, was created with an image link, the only way to disable it was to get rid of the `href` attribute:

```
<a><img src="disabled-first-page.gif" alt="First Page"/></a>
<a><img src="disabled-prev-page.gif" alt="Previous Page"/></a>
```

It is an ugly hack.

Now, we can use the ARIA `disabled` attribute:

```
<span role="button" aria-disabled="true" id="FirstButton">
<img src="disabled-first-page.gif" alt="First Page"/>
</span>
```

Here's an example of an input element from the Dojo Toolkit. The code is for the text area after the text `onChange:`. Note the different syntax when dealing with Dojo—`disabled` doesn't require a name/value pair:

```
<input id="oc1" disabled value="not fired yet!" autocomplete="off">
```

Figure 9-3 shows a screenshot of this form.

Figure 9-3. Screenshot of disabled input area from http://archive.dojotoolkit.org/nightly/ dojotoolkit/dijit/tests/form/test_Spinner.html

Maintaining relationships

As you create new nodes and add them to the DOM, make sure you add them at an appropriate place or use `aria-owns` to create a meaningful reading order.[†]

> [T]he DOM enables assistive technologies to request the "parent" of the object on which the user is working. However, the DOM hierarchy is acyclic—each node may have one and only one parent, making it impossible to represent all parent/child relationships within a single hierarchy. An example is a `treeitem`. Here, the user often asks for the container parent such as a folder name. In rich Internet applications, only a subset of treeitems may be available at any one time, and they may be added dynamically without modification to the DOM tree hierarchy—a common occurrence in Ajax applications.
>
> Using `aria-owns` in the following example, the `"dropbox"` div is explicitly identified as a child of the `"mine"` div, even though `"dropbox"` is not an actual child in the DOM. WAI-ARIA calls `"dropbox"` an *adopted* child.
>
> —WAI-ARIA Best Practices, Section 5.2.1

```
<div role="treeitem" aria-owns="mine">My Documents<div>
...
<div id="dropbox" role="group">
  <div role="treeitem">Chapter 1</div>
  <div role="treeitem">Chapter 2</div>
</div>
```

Summary

Ajax and WAI-ARIA represent an exciting area rich with potential for innovation. The similar constraints on viewport size and lack of a mouse create an overlap of needs and techniques for mobile and accessible design.

[†] *http://www.w3.org/WAI/PF/aria-practices/#relations_owning*

Rich Internet Applications

With great power comes great responsibility.

—From a Spider-Man comic in Marvel's
Amazing Fantasy #15

So far in this book, we've been talking about web applications that are mostly web-, that is, HTML-based. But we can't forget that the Web does contain software in the form of Flash, Java, and now Silverlight. These platforms have advantages and challenges all their own where universal design is concerned, and in this chapter, we cover them.

Now that the Web has begun to act like software, web accessibility comprises software accessibility. While we might have expected from the head start we had with software design that loads of software accessibility documentation would be here waiting for us, sadly, that part has not come to pass. There is not a corpus of software accessibility best practices that we can rely on—no books that we can recommend, no WCAG-like list of checkpoints. So in this chapter, we offer a crash course in software accessibility as applied to Flex and Silverlight.

The software accessibility guidelines that do exist need a refresh based on changes in languages and devices. Even then, it would be very difficult for any set of guidelines to address everything you can do with software in such the way WCAG 1.0 can do with HTML, or WCAG 2.0 tries to do across web technologies. For general Human Interface Guidelines, refer to *http://en.wiki pedia.org/wiki/Human_interface_guidelines*.

It should be noted that Java, the granddaddy of Internet applications, does have its own accessibility API, as well as a package called the Java Access Bridge, which lets Windows assistive technologies connect to it. However, Java is an expansive and complex language, and so covering Java accessibility would be a book unto itself; and Sun's RIA project, JavaFX, was still in the planning stages at the time this book was published, so the Java accessibility stack is not covered in this book. We recommend Sun's own documentation, available at *http://www.sun.com/accessibility/*.

Features of RIAs

Macromedia (now Adobe, which is, by the way of full disclosure, Matt's employer) coined the term *Rich Internet Applications* (RIAs) to refer to apps that access data over the network and offer a user experience that HTML can't match. Conveniently enough, it also created a platform called Flex around that time to attract developers more familiar with XML and integrated development environments such as Eclipse than the drawing tools, timelines, and stage native to the Flash authoring tool. The ability to create and distribute components that worked in the ubiquitous Flash Player opened up the world to some of the most innovative—and conversely, some of the most unusable—user experiences the Web has seen.

Microsoft has begun targeting the same RIA market with Silverlight. Both have similarities that set them apart from traditional software and web development:

- User interfaces are built in an XML-based language (MXML for Flex, XAML for Silverlight).
- Developers can use components bundled with the runtime or develop their own from scratch.
- Data access components offer connectivity to hosts using SOAP, XML over HTTP, or a variety of other protocols.
- Developers can control the visual experience to a greater extent than they could using either HTML, or older widget toolkits such as Swing or Windows Forms.
- Audio and video playback is native in each platform.
- Unlike HTML, content in Flex and Silverlight is compiled code, and Flex and Silverlight applications on every platform offer the same (or a very similar) look and feel.

The potential for a better cross-platform user experience has never been greater. But as we've learned from Spider-Man, it's up to us as developers to use that power for the greater good.

Although WCAG 2.0 was designed to include guidance relevant to platforms such as Flash and Silverlight, it only goes so far when you are looking at how to offer accessibility programmatically. Each platform has an accessibility API of its own, and the developer is responsible for enabling that API and testing with assistive technology and evaluation tools to ensure that it is working properly with actual users. We discuss the tools we use later on in the chapter.

The runtimes themselves, on the other hand, fall under the purview of the User Agent Accessibility Guidelines (UAAG). This, the least known of the three W3C/WAI guidelines documents, outlines how a "user agent" (defined as a browser, plug-in, or media player either alone or in conjunction with an assistive technology) needs to behave when it is rendering content. But content can be a tricky thing. In UAAG, content is referred to primarily as an object representing a document.

Wait. Where's the document object in Flex or Silverlight? There are XML files, sure, but they actually represent ActionScript or .NET code, not a document in the same sense as we find in HTML and web browsers. UAAG does make a lot of sense for HTML user agents and even other kinds of content in the Flash Player. But when we talk about applications, we're still left wanting for guidance.

Mobile RIAs have a different problem: they are only now becoming possible. In March 2008, Microsoft announced that a mobile version of Silverlight would ship on Nokia S60 phone and Internet Tablet devices, as well as the older Series 40. Adobe doesn't currently ship a version of Flash Lite that can run Flex, but Flash Player 9 already works with Flex on the Internet Tablets.

It's only a matter of time before both of these platforms will support mobile devices. When they do, though, they will each need to guide users on how to develop components that will work well on each hardware platform. For example, if you have a weather application that runs full-screen on your desktop, how will that translate to your phone, which is 320x240, or less? It may be possible to have one package that will run on both, but the interface will need to be adaptive and that will require the runtime to do a lot of the heavy lifting. We believe that the principles of universal design will soon be practicable between desktop and mobile software applications, but it will take at least a couple more years before that convergence can begin.

Assistive Technology Support for RIAs

Flash Player and Silverlight contain accessibility APIs that connect to the operating system's API (that is, if it happens to be Windows). Here's a basic overview of the state of OS-level accessibility interfaces.

Microsoft Active Accessibility (MSAA) was introduced in Windows 95 as a means of exposing information about the role and state of Windows controls to assistive technology. It consists of an interface called IAccessible, which can be attached to user interface controls and updated with the current role and state.

In Windows Vista, Microsoft introduced a new accessibility-related API called User Interface Automation (UIA). It was built separately from MSAA and was designed for .Net applications, including the Windows Presentation Framework (WPF), which Silverlight is based on. Novell is porting UIA to Linux.

There's another API called IAccessible2 (or IA2), which has taken a more incremental approach than UIA. As its name implies, IA2 builds on top of the MSAA IAccessible interface in Windows. IA2 has also been ported to Linux and is implemented in Firefox 3 on both platforms.

We focus on MSAA here for two reasons: it covers the core of all software accessibility design, and to date, it is the only broadly supported accessibility API. Over time, this will change, but a decent understanding of MSAA is necessary both now and into the future in order to handle software accessibility.

Other accessibility APIs

The two other accessibility APIs you should know about are Apple's NSAccessibility and the Linux AT-SPI interface. They each offer platform-level accessibility roughly comparable to what MSAA, IA2, or UIA offer on Windows.

What you need to know about these APIs is that, at least at this time, RIA platform vendors do not support either very well, and there are no plans for accessibility API support at this time for any of the platforms we're discussing. Direct accessibility remains almost exclusively Windows territory for the time being.

Flex Accessibility

Now let's get back to the action.

We can't talk about Flex without talking about Flash Player, as it's the engine that runs Flex code. The same is true for Flex accessibility: it borrows its functionality from the Flash Player accessibility API. The first version of Flash Player to support MSAA was version 6 in 2002. In order to make a Flash movie accessible, though, you needed to do a lot of custom work in ActionScript, the JavaScript-based language at the core of every Flash object.

It is possible to write what you might call a web application using Flash without adopting Flex, but there really aren't many good reasons to do so. The Flash authoring tool is geared to designers and consigns ActionScript code to a single panel, while Flex Builder is an Eclipse-based IDE built for coders. Flash authors

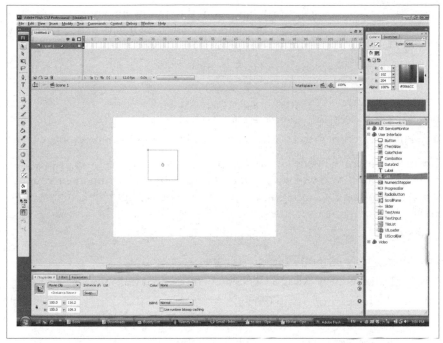

Figure 10-1. The stage

care about timelines and libraries of graphics; Flex authors care about debuggers and libraries of code. That's not to say anything bad about the Flash environment or its users, but it is not and was never designed for full-time software developers.

The most important difference, as far as we're concerned, is what it takes to make Flash objects accessible compared to Flex components. Let's say you're in Adobe Flash CS3 Professional and you want to add a listbox. Here are the steps to do it:

1. From the Components panel, select the CheckBox component and drag it onto the stage.
2. In the Parameters panel, set the Label value to Organic.
3. Now select the List component and drag it onto the stage, as shown in Figure 10-1.
4. Under Properties, name your object "lstFruits".
5. Go to the Parameters panel, click on dataProviders, and add a few items to your list.

6. Go to the Actions panel, and add the following code to add the `AccessibilityImplementation` object, which contains the code necessary to make the `List` and `CheckBox` components accessible:

```
import fl.accessibility.ListAccImpl;
ListAccImpl.enableAccessibility();

import fl.accessibility.CheckBoxAccImpl;
CheckBoxAccImpl.enableAccessibility();
```

7. Publish a preview to HTML, and view it in a Windows-based browser.

If you have more than one kind of component, as you are likely to in a real-life web application, you will have to repeat step 4 for each component you use. This can be time-consuming and unwieldy, of course, but failing to do so will leave your components inaccessible.

Now, here's how you do it in Flex Builder 3:

1. Make sure your project is set to enable accessibility.
2. In the design view, drag a CheckBox component onto the stage.
3. Set the Label property to Organic.
4. Drag a List component onto the stage.
5. Under Properties, name your object "lstFruits".
6. In the code view, add the following code inside the XML block Flex Builder created for you:

```
<mx:List id="lstFruits">
    <mx:dataProvider>
        <mx:Array>
            <mx:Object label="Apple" data="001" />
            <mx:Object label="Banana" data="002"/>
            <mx:Object label="Orange" data="003"/>
        </mx:Array>
    </mx:dataProvider>
</mx:List>
```

7. Now build this code and run it in a browser.

It may be the same number of steps, but on the scale of a real application, it's much less work to make the same kinds of content accessible in Flex.

Creating the Look: Accessible Custom Components

As with Ajax, the first step is to look at existing controls to see if there is one that is similar to what you need. You can then reuse the semantics and behaviors and tweak them as necessary, while inheriting any accessibility behaviors that have been built-in.

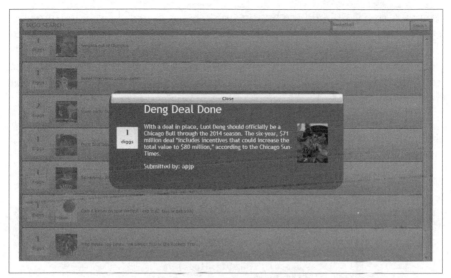

Figure 10-2. Pop-up of story details overlays list of search results

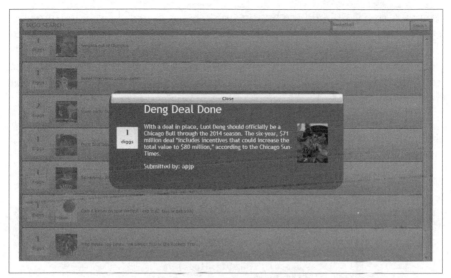

Figure 10-3. An instance of MyButton with 3 diggs, an icon, and text

Wendy recently tweaked a sample Digg search application, which we'll use as the basis of a case study. We're going to discuss various decisions made during the process and how those decisions relate to universal design. The application has three main processes:

1. Enter a search term.
2. Display Digg search results.
3. Select a search result for more information about the story.

First, we'll focus on the story results. We decided to make each story a button because we want to navigate through the list of buttons (with the arrow keys, the Tab key, or the mouse), and then select a story. More information about the story will be displayed in a pop-up, as shown in Figure 10-2.

Button is a good choice because assistive technologies are familiar with buttons and know that a button means you can invoke it and something will happen. We can already tab to buttons and depending on which type of container we use, we will probably inherit arrow key behaviors as well.

The next step is to build the buttons in such a way that the relationships between them can be identified. In Silverlight, there are a few containers to
choose from; DataGrid and List are the most obvious choices. DataGrid is a
good first choice, but the semantics aren't quite right. We have only one
column of data—it would be similar to using a single column table to lay out
a web page. Instead, the list seems to be the best solution.

Silverlight uses XAML to create the visual appearance of interface objects. For
example, the following XAML creates a button that has a yellow Digg box, a
thumbnail, and the title of the story:

```
<Digg:MyButton Click="Button_Click">
  <Digg:MyButton.Content>
    <StackPanel Orientation="Horizontal">

      <!-- Yellow Digg Panel with NumDiggs-->
      <StackPanel Style="{StaticResource DiggPanel}">
        <TextBlock Text="{Binding NumDiggs}"
         Style="{StaticResource NumDigsBlock}"/>
        <TextBlock Text="diggs"
         Style="{StaticResource NumDigsSubBlock}"/>
      </StackPanel>

      <!-- Story Thumbnail Preview -->
      <Image Source="{Binding ThumbNail}"
       Style="{StaticResource ThumbNailPreview}"/>

      <!-- Story Title-->
      <TextBlock Text="{Binding Title}" Margin="5"
       Style="{StaticResource TitleBlock}"/>

    </StackPanel>
  </Digg:MyButton.Content>
</Digg:MyButton>
```

Figure 10-3 shows an instance of the MyButton class.

Note the use of MyButton—this is a custom class that extends the Button class.
Button isn't used "as is" because we want to add an Automation Peer that
allows us to control how the UIA properties are exposed. In this case, we set
the name of the control to contain all of the strings inside it. A peer, which is
owned by the primary control, contains additional information and is created
when an Automation Client is listening to the application.

Some UIA properties can be set in XAML, but when populating controls on
the fly, you need a "template" that can be created over and over for each Digg
story. Because of this need for flexibility, it was easiest to create a new class.

The goal is for all of the information presented visually on the button to be
presented to an assistive technology. In this case, after we created the visual
appearance of the button in XAML, we need to set additional UIA properties

in the *code behind*, here C#, used to add behavior to the custom control. We need to override the GetNameCore method, in effect creating the text equivalent for this button:

```
protected override string GetNameCore()
{
  MyButton button = (MyButton)this.Owner;
  DiggStory story = (DiggStory)button.DataContext;
  return story.Title + " " + story.NumDiggs + " diggs";
}
```

We can confirm this works with the Visual UIA Verifier (VIV) tools, as seen in Figure 10-4.

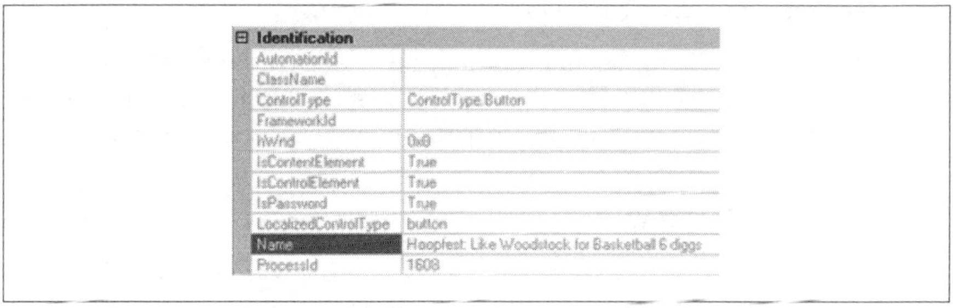

Figure 10-4. Testing that name is properly set for an instance of MyButton

Creating the Feel: Accessible Custom Components

With Ajax, when constructing custom controls from scratch, you need to implement all of the keyboard support for those controls unless you use a toolkit that has implemented keyboard support in the widgets. Both Flex and Silverlight offer basic keyboard navigation support for their widget libraries. However, these methods usually need to be tweaked to get the exact experience you are looking for, and sometimes focus doesn't move between components as expected.

Here is the behavior that we want:

1. The user tabs to the Search button and presses Return.
2. A list of stories is displayed.
3. The user presses Tab to give focus to the list of stories.
4. The user presses Enter to get more details about a story.
5. A pop-up is displayed with story details.
6. The user presses Return to close the window.
7. The user is returned to the list of stories and continues navigating.

Out of the box, tabbing between components and button presses works as desired, but focus does not move to the pop-up window.

As with JavaScript and Ajax, the event handlers are not device-specific. Instead of using keyboard- or mouse-specific events, we're listening for the "click" event on buttons, which will fire either on a mouse press or an Enter keypress.

We've been building on code from a Silverlight tutorial (*http://weblogs.asp.net/ scottgu/pages/silverlight-tutorial-part-6-using-user-controls-to-implement-mas ter-detail-scenarios.aspx*), in which Microsoft's Scott Guthrie uses a list with an event listener on `SelectionChanged`. For keyboard users, that means each time they navigate in the list, details for the previous story pop up. To fix this, we changed the type of list container (in the XAML) and moved the event handlers to the buttons themselves.

Navigating between components was an issue. Focus did not move from the components as expected. When the pop-up was displayed, we had to specifically move focus from the current story to the pop-up's close button.

Backend Considerations

The purpose of RIAs is to deliver data. Usually, this is done similarly to the Ajax model: bits of XML are passed to the client at certain intervals or in response to certain user actions.

In the following example, we use the Digg API to search for stories matching a given keyword, in this case, "basketball." Here's an example of the XML we receive for a story. Note that the thumbnail element does not contain a description of the image.

```
<story id="7298020" link="http://ballersnetwork.com/p/en/ballers/
spokane-hoopfest-day-1/" submit_date="1214921190" diggs="6" comments="1"
status="upcoming" media="news" href="http://digg.com/basketball/Hoopfest_
Like_Woodstock_for_Basketball">
  <title>Hoopfest: Like Woodstock for Basketball</title>
  <description>The world's largest 3-on-3 tournament invaded downtown
Spokane this weekend, with hundreds of hoops taking over the roads and
shutting downtown down. Pacific Northwest loves their bball –
which makes the departure of the Sonics that much sadder.</description>
  <user name="freedomjenkins" icon="http://digg.com/users/freedomjenkins/l.png"
registered="1174186547" profileviews="219" fullname="Freedom Jenkins" />
  <topic name="Basketball" short_name="basketball" />
  <container name="Sports" short_name="sports" />
  <thumbnail originalwidth="651" originalheight="658"
contentType="image/jpeg"src="http://digg.com/basketball/
Hoopfest_Like_Woodstock_for_Basketball/t.jpg" width="80" height="80" />
</story>
```

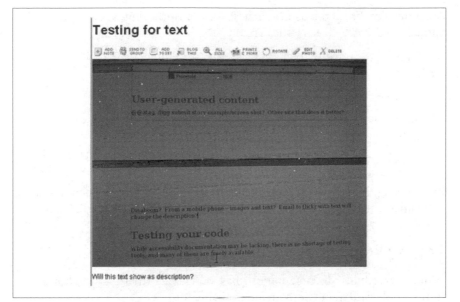

Figure 10-5. A screenshot of Flickr's page for a photo uploaded from a mobile phone

The ideal authoring scenario, according to what we know about WCAG and ATAG, would be:

1. The Digg API has an `alt` attribute on the thumbnail element.
2. When submitting a story, Digg's form asks for a short description for each thumbnail.
3. We receive the `alt` attribute along with the rest of the information and dynamically associate the text with the image.

Since that wasn't the case, and we couldn't generate a text equivalent for each image, we assumed that the thumbnail did not contain important information and we could mark it as a decorative artifact and thus something to ignore. The name of the button concatenates the story's title and number of diggs, instead of creating three separate components.

User-Generated Content

Make it easy for users to generate accessible content. For example, Flickr allows users to upload photos from mobile phones via email. The subject of the email is used as the title for the photo and any text in the body is used for description, as shown in Figure 10-5.

Digg could do something similar on its "story submission" page—not only asking for a thumbnail but also its alt text. Guidance on prompting users to generate accessible code is available from the Authoring Tools Accessibility Guidelines 2.0. The basic issues are:

- Support the creation of accessible content (Guideline B.1.1).
- Preserve accessible content as it's added (Guideline B.1.2).
- Generate accessible content (Guideline B.1.3).
- Make the most accessible option the easiest one for the user to choose (Guideline B.3.1).
- Prompt for and store alternate content for nontext objects (Guideline B.2.4).
- Show authors how to create accessible content with your documentation and any templates you provide (Guideline B.2.5, Guideline B.3.5).

Testing Your Code

While accessibility documentation may be lacking, there is no shortage of testing tools, and many of them are available for free.

Microsoft Testing Tools

Microsoft offers a number of free tools to check MSAA accessibility. The most useful everyday applications are inspect32 and AccExplorer32.

Perhaps the best way to visualize the inner workings of the MSAA stack is using the navigator in AccExplorer. Dragging the compass icon over objects on the screen shows you how items are grouped, and you can find out everything associated with that object, from name and description, to role and state, to keyboard shortcut.

For UIA, the UISpy and Visual UIA Verifier (VIV) tools have similar functionality. See Figure 10-4 (shown earlier) for a VIV screenshot. Figure 10-6 shows "Swarm"—a Flash application that creates a swarm in real time based on current Digg activity. The inset is a screenshot from inspect32 looking at one of the stories.

Using inspect32 you see the MSAA fields that an assistive technology uses to generate an interface. The primary fields to note are Name, Role, State, Description, DefAction (for "default action," or what happens when the object is actuated), Parent, and Children.

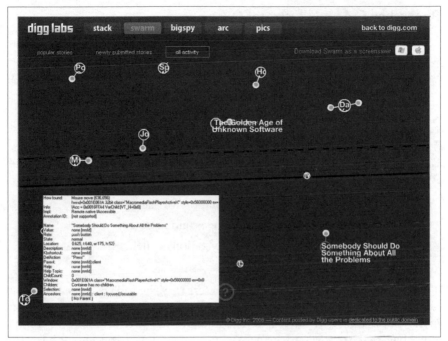

Figure 10-6. Screenshot of "Swarm"

ACTF

A newer toolset is the Accessibility Tools Framework (ACTF). These tools run in the Eclipse development environment on Windows and a couple are of interest to the RIA developer.

AccProbe and aDesigner

The AccProbe tool is designed to combine the functionality of all of Microsoft's accessibility testing tools—inspect32, AccExplorer, and AccEvent—while adding support for IA2. It's still in development, but it already does a reasonably good job replacing these tools.

Another tool in the suite takes accessibility testing to another level. Using aDesigner, you can test your application using a series of filters that emulate various types of visual impairment. aDesigner supports HTML, Flash, and the OpenOffice ODF format, and produces a score.

Photoshop CS4 and Illustrator CS4

Lastly, Adobe Photoshop CS4 and Illustrator CS4 contain a feature that allows users to view an image as people with the most common forms of colorblindness (protanopia and deuteranopia) do. These options are under the View→Proof Setup menu.

Summary

Rich Internet Applications have many things in common with JavaScript- and Ajax-based web applications:

- Provide role, state, and name information for each control
- Guarantee users are notified of changes and updates
- Create meaningful structure and navigation sequences
- Ensure keyboard-only operation

The difference lies in the ability of RIAs to create richer objects. We hope that universal design will be baked into any toolkit a developer chooses to use, but in more cases than not, you will need to take extra steps to ensure accessibility. We hope that the overlap in needs and constraints between mobile and accessibility design will drive developers to take these additional steps.

The Process

Most of the web accessibility success stories are attributable to evangelists within an organization. It is one thing to have a corporate policy that dictates accessibility as a requirement and another thing to execute it. Often, sites are made accessible not as a result of an order from the top but by people who are "just doing their job" within the web team —especially folks who understand that even the best automated tools are no replacement for good design.

Universal by Design

All too often, organizations *begin* to think about accessibility near the end of a project. Unfortunately, that's usually too late. Universal design is not just a checkbox—it is a discipline that should be included in the original specifications of a product, site, or application; and revisited throughout the development, refining, and launch of an application. If UD is left to chance, the time and cost involved in reworking what you've already done increases dramatically.

We have made frequent mention of guidelines such as the Web Content Accessibility Guidelines and the Mobile Web Best Practices. It's necessary for any stakeholder group to state their needs as clearly as possible and how to satisfy them. And because the audience for these documents is both international and made up of people with differing skill levels, the guidance they provide is as simple as they can make it. In the case of WCAG, it's even transformed in various ways to speak to managers, developers, testers, and browser and authoring tool vendors; and reconstituted in every form from business case to primer to business card. In fact, you may consider this book another one of these remixes.

However, as we've also learned throughout the book, the proof is in the pudding. Taking a hyper-literal view of any set of checkpoints can hurt as much as it helps, particularly when the people using them don't understand how or why they apply. If we understand guidelines documents for what they are—an expression of potential problems and solutions—we can then adapt our own content, and our own processes, to produce the best content we can offer.

Tools and Testing

In this context, automated tools lose even more of their luster. A number of companies are out there telling potential customers that their products will do all the heavy lifting for them, checking content against WCAG or Section 508 and pointing to what needs to be done, or even repairing them automatically. There is a whole laundry list of reasons why that logic doesn't hold up.

If guidelines are a shorthand expression of the problem, then evaluation tools are machine algorithms that attempt to identify violations of those guidelines. That amounts to two degrees of separation from the original problem set. Put those results in front of someone who doesn't understand them and you're playing a game of telephone with your authoring process.

Here's what happens when you rely on tools to replace the judgment of trained content producers:

- Evaluating content moves to the very end of the process, which means bad markup practices survive long enough to be expensive and difficult, if not impossible, to repair. This perpetuates the stereotype, particularly common among content producers, that accessibility is too costly to implement.

- Freed of the responsibility of thinking of how the content will actually be used, the focus shifts to doing all that is necessary to silence the tool. At times, this can and does cause authors to add code that actually harms accessibility, simply to reduce the number of errors the tool emits. Here's a classic example that drives screen-reader users *nuts*:

    ```
    <img src="blank.gif" alt="This image is for visual
    presentation only">
    ```

- No algorithm is fully automatic. Each evaluation tool emits numerous manual checks, which often represent critical requirements. But while tools assume the manual checks have been completed when they state a document conforms to a given standard, those checks are almost never done. And if the evaluator is a novice, she may not even know where to begin if she wanted to do them.

While you may not hear this from some of the sales teams pushing these products, some developers of these evaluation and repair tools will readily acknowledge their limits. That's not to say that automated tools can't help. Like any tool—think scalpels, jackhammers, or blowtorches—professionals can use them with outstanding results, while amateurs can use them with outcomes ranging from mildly harmful to catastrophic.

Development Tools

Any time you attempt to introduce any kind of rigor to your processes, you will want to have tools that help you stick to it rather than get in your way.

As the first web accessibility techniques were springing up, developers had begun to complain that their authoring tools were deleting anything that they had added to the documents they were editing simply because the tools didn't understand anything they didn't generate.

In part out of that frustration, the W3C/WAI Authoring Tool Accessibility Guidelines (ATAG) were born. ATAG contains a list of guidelines and techniques both similar in style and complementary in content to WCAG. Just as importantly, it gives concrete guidance to authoring tool developers on how to make it easier to create accessible content, evaluate it for usability by people with disabilities, and repair accessibility problems as they're introduced. Looking for tools that support accessibility will make your life both as a content producer and as an aggregator of others' content significantly easier—not pain-free, of course, but every little bit helps.

It is unlikely that you will find *one* tool to do everything; over time, you will have a variety of tools. How you use those tools will change over time...not to mention that new tools are coming out every day.

Content management systems (CMSs)

Maybe the most important genre of authoring tool available today is the content management system. Millions of web authors use CMSs, including blogging software, to ply their trade—and many if not most of those folks have never touched a line of HTML code in their lives. For that reason alone, the makeup of your CMS is key to the best practices of universal design.

ATAG has important requirements for CMSs to enable them to create and manage accessible content. For example, ATAG-conforming content management systems will ensure that all that metadata and semantic table markup you created won't be lost when it's added to the repository. Conforming tools will come with templates that already meet WCAG requirements. They will check your content for accessibility problems, and provide assistance in

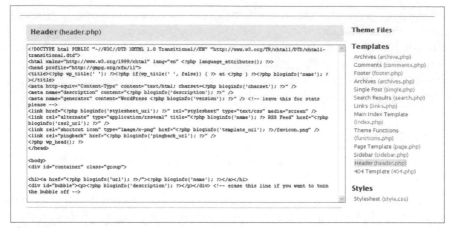

Figure 11-1. *WordPress Theme Editor—adding lang attribute to html element*

repairing them. And they will allow people with disabilities to create and maintain content themselves.

Building and managing templates

Depending on the CMS you choose, "building" a template may be more like "modifying an existing one." For example, the WordPress Theme Directory (*http://wordpress.org/extend/themes/*) has 170 themes to choose from. After you choose and install a theme, you can use the Theme Editor to modify it.

You'll want to see the template in action to determine if it produces accessible results and then modify the themes so that they produce acceptable output. For example, Wendy recently installed the Journalist template from Lucian E. Marin. Using the UD4WA 20 Questions, we found a few issues with the template that we needed to fix to ensure that Wendy's blog conformed with WCAG 2.0 Level A. The human language was not specified for the blog. While it is probably more appropriate to set the language in one of the WordPress configuration files, editing the Header template in the Theme viewer, as shown in Figure 11-1, does the trick.

Third-party and user-contributed content

Now that we've identified and fixed errors with the template, let's customize it. Let's start by adding del.icio.us and twitter badges—when Wendy bookmarks a site or tweets, the updates automatically appear on her blog, keeping it fresh between blog posts. Running the site through the W3C HTML and CSS validators, we found validation errors with both badges.

Figure 11-2 is both an example of the problem and the fix. &count=5 uses an ampersand, which in HTML indicates an entity reference. The W3C Markup Validation Service explains:

> Entity references start with an ampersand (&) and end with a semicolon (;). If you want to use a literal ampersand in your document you must encode it as "&" (even inside URLs!). Be careful to end entity references with a semicolon or your entity reference may get interpreted in connection with the following text.

Therefore, the previous variable in the URI, &icon=m, is properly marked and passes the validator. The fix for the twitter badge is replacing the use of the embed element with the object element (à la Drew McLellan's Flash Satay method). Fixes are applied via the WordPress Theme Editor.

With every change you make to your site, you'll have to test that it works as expected. This also includes testing for accessibility.

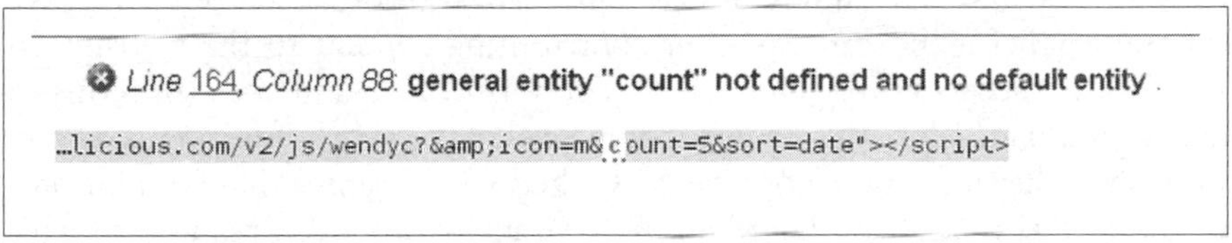

⊗ *Line 164, Column 88:* **general entity "count" not defined and no default entity** .

…licious.com/v2/js/wendyc?&icon=m&count=5&sort=date"></script>

Figure 11-2. Results of running WordPress blog with del.icio.us badge through the W3C Markup Validation Service

Mash-ups, repurposing, and community contributions

One of the beautiful (and really fun) aspects of the proliferation of Web 2.0 applications is the ability to reuse data in different contexts; for example, you can use "blog this" in Flickr to create a post on Blogger. You might think that Flickr has enough information about an image for Blogger to fill in the alt attribute on the image element, but unfortunately, it publishes an image with it empty, alt="":

```
<a href=http://www.flickr.com/photos/sp1ral/2626500479/
title="photo sharing">
<img src="http://farm4.static.flickr.com/
3184/2626500479_7e16ecb380_m.jpg" alt=""
style="border: solid 2px #000000;" /></a>
```

The link to the image at Flickr is followed by a title (which is another link to the image) and a link to the photographer's Flickr photostream:

```
<br /><span style="font-size: 0.9em; margin-top:0px;"><a
href="http://www.flickr.com/photos/sp1ral/2626500479/">1st radish</a>
<br />Originally uploaded by <a href=
"http://www.flickr.com/people/sp1ral/">
anneke boudreau</a></span>
```

Again, you'll need to continually evaluate the results that are produced and either fix the problems by hand or create processes that will make the fixes for you. Another option is to work with the service provider and make it more accessible for everyone. Chances are you are not alone—and if enough people request the fix, it is more likely to be made. Or, make your own interface that grabs the data from the service and provides it in an alternative format—like Easy SlideShare (*http://icant.co.uk/easy-slideshare/about/*).

Training and maintaining

Your site can be a funnel for information coming from a variety of sources. After you learn and employ accessibility practices, you aren't finished. You will need to ensure that new widgets or add-ons that you add to your site, changes to the CMS, and other factors don't break the universal design you've mastered.

As we'll discuss later, different sizes (and types) of organizations will have different policies and processes for contributing content to the website. In some cases, access is very controlled. The most successful sites (in terms of accessibility) are those that require some level of training before someone can publish to the site. One school we've worked with requires that content producers attend a class. Another requires that content producers read Ian Lloyd's *Build Your Own Website the Right Way* (SitePoint). Organizations that have a policy and actively raise the awareness about it and how to meet it have the most accessible sites. Organizations that have a policy but are not proactive about educating or raising awareness about it fall somewhere in the middle of the spectrum. An unfortunate reality is that organizations that don't have an accessibility policy usually don't have accessible sites.

Evaluation Tools and Resources

The tools and resources that we include in the following discussion are a mere sample of what is available. For a searchable database of available tools, please consult the Web Accessibility Initiative's overview at *http://www.w3.org/WAI/ER/tools/Overview*.

WAT

The Web Accessibility Toolbar (WAT) is available for Internet Explorer and Opera from the Web Accessibility Tools Consortium (*http://www.wat-c.org/tools/*).

Since it's in the toolbar, it's one of the first places we turn when evaluating a site. It doesn't make any judgments about the accessibility of a site—it provides you with a variety of reports that allow you to determine if a site or application has issues.

Jim Thatcher provides a good overview of the toolbar and its functions at *http://www.jimthatcher.com/news-061507.htm*, and The University of Washington's Draft Web Accessibility Rubric walks you through an evaluation using the WAT (*http://staff.washington.edu/tft/rubric.php*).

WAVE 4.0

WAVE is a service that can be run from any browser and is also available as a toolbar for Firefox. Instead of providing a report, it embeds icons within a web page indicating potential issues. It's available from WebAIM at *http://wave .webaim.org/*.

A good place to start is "Introducing WAVE 4.0": *http://www.webaim.org/ blog/introducing-wave-4/*.

Firebug

If you are debugging JavaScript or CSS, you'll want Firebug—a Firefox add-on. Download it here at *https://addons.mozilla.org/en-US/firefox/addon/1843*.

As with other debugging tools, you can set breakpoints, step through code, and watch the values of variables and objects. The "Layout" inspector allows you to see offset, margin, border, padding, height, and width for any object on a page.

Links to tutorials and other resources are available at *http://en.wikipedia.org/ wiki/Firebug_(Firefox_extension)*.

W3C validation tools

The W3C provides a variety of tools that check the syntax of HTML and CSS:

- W3C Markup Validation Service (*http://validator.w3.org/*)
- W3C CSS Validation Service (*http://jigsaw.w3.org/css-validator/*)
- W3C mobileOK Checker (*http://validator.w3.org/mobile/*)

W3C also provides a link checker, RSS checker (Feed Validator), and RDF Validator. More information about W3C tools is available at *http://www.w3 .org/QA/Tools/*.

inspect32

inspect32 is one of Microsoft's Active Accessibility 2.0 SDK Tools (*http://ti nyurl.com/88adk*).

You use it to check name, role, state, and other properties of Flash/Flex, Silverlight, and Ajax objects. It's a window into the information provided via Microsoft's Active Accessibility (MSAA) to assistive technologies.

Accessibility Probe and Accerciser

Accessibility Probe (AccProbe) is similar to inspect32 except it uses a richer set of accessibility APIs to gather information. As we've mentioned before, MSAA was the gold standard in accessibility APIs until recently. AccProbe communicates with IAccessible2, which some of the WAI-ARIA implementations use, and continues to use MSAA for basic desktop widgets. Find it at *http://www.eclipse.org/actf/downloads/*.

If you're using the GNOME desktop, check out Accerciser at *http://live.gnome .org/Accerciser*.

Browsers

More than likely, you are already testing your sites/applications in a variety of browsers—Firefox, Internet Explorer, and Safari (WebKit) at least. Opera should be in that list as well. Be sure to keep track of browser usage statistics and continue testing older versions. Usage share statistics vary by source, but the current trend seems to be that Internet Explorer usage is split between versions 6, 7, and 8. Considering that IE6 has so many...issues...it is wise to keep a copy around for testing.

You can operate all of these browsers via the keyboard. Try it out. The most basic task is pressing Tab to jump to the next link (Shift+Tab to go backward) and Enter to activate the current link. While you're at it, check out the other accessibility features. Here are some resources to get you started:

- Accessibility Features in Firefox (includes links to add-ons) (*http://www .mozilla.org/access/features*).
- The Mozilla Community runs AccessFirefox, a great resource for all things related to accessibility and Firefox (*http://www.accessfirefox.org/*), including a list of keyboard shortcuts (*http://www.accessfirefox.org/Firefox_Key board_and_Mouse_Shortcuts.html*).
- Accessibility Features in Internet Explorer 7 (*http://www.microsoft.com/ enable/products/ie7/*).
- The Keyboard Lover's Guide to IE7 (*http://blogs.msdn.com/ie/archive/ 2006/02/08/527702.aspx*).
- What's New for Accessibility in Internet Explorer 8 (*http://msdn.microsoft .com/en-us/library/cc304059(VS.85).aspx*).

- (Keyboard Shortcuts) Quick Reference Guide: (*http://www.microsoft.com/windows/products/winfamily/ie/quickref.mspx*).
- Accessibility in Opera (*http://www.opera.com/products/desktop/access/*).
- Use Opera Without a Mouse (*http://www.opera.com/support/tutorials/nomouse/*).
- Accessibility in The WebKit Open Source Project.

  As of this writing, the accessibility features of WebKit are not yet documented, but a placeholder exists at *http://webkit.org/projects/accessibility/index.html*.

 Google's Chrome was released as we were finalizing this book. Steve Faulkner whipped up this quick overview of the initial look at Chrome accessibility: *http://www.paciellogroup.com/blog/?p=92*.

System accessibility

Most operating systems have accessibility features built-in—including keyboard support, mouse emulation, and high-contrast display modes. In some cases, assistive technologies are being built into the system, as the Linux Foundation is doing. Here is a list of system accessibility resources:

- Apple Accessibility (includes Mac OSX and iPhone) (*http://www.apple.com/accessibility/*)
- The Linux Foundation Accessibility (*http://www.linuxfoundation.org/en/Accessibility*)
- Accessibility in Windows Vista (*http://www.microsoft.com/enable/products/windowsvista/*)
- Windows XP Accessibility Resources (*http://www.microsoft.com/enable/products/windowsxp/default.aspx*)

Screen readers

Using your site with a screen reader and the monitor turned off is an eye-opening experience <groan/>. It's a bad joke, but it's true. Eyes-free, keyboard-only operation of a site is a completely different experience. Be sure to learn the basic keystrokes for each screen reader. Unfortunately, they are all different. For the screen readers that we don't use as often, we keep cheat sheets tacked to the wall. After you get the hang of it, the keystrokes become second nature—like editing a document in Emacs. Even after using the other tools to inspect the code, we always pick up something new when using a screen reader.

If you are developing an application that runs outside of a browser sandbox, you'll need to test with a standalone screen reader. The following are a few screen readers from which to choose:

- Jaws ($895, standalone) (*http://www.freedomscientific.com/fs_downloads/ jaws.asp*)
- FireVox (free, Firefox add-on) (*http://firevox.clcworld.net/*)
- Hal (£575, free demo, standalone) (*http://www.yourdolphin.com/product detail.asp?id=5*)
- NVDA (free, standalone) (*http://www.nvda-project.org/*)
- Orca (free, standalone) (*http://live.gnome.org/Orca*)
- WebAnywhere (free, standalone) (*http://webanywhere.cs.washington .edu/*)

The following are links to some videos of people using screen readers. These are helpful, allowing you to watch someone talk through his experience on a site:

- Neal Ewers—Introduction to the Screen Reader (6 minutes) (*http://www .doit.wisc.edu/accessibility/video/intro.asp*)
- Victor Tsaran—An Introduction to Screen Readers (26 minutes) (*http:// video.yahoo.com/watch/514676/2686894*)
- Surfing the Web with a Screen Reader (22 minutes; $10; free sample clip) (*http://www.washington.edu/accessit/surfing.php*)

Magnification

The most popular magnifier at the moment is the iPhone. Most browsers now offer magnification (Opera has had it for several years). As with screen readers, if you are developing an application that runs outside of a browser sandbox, you'll need to test with a standalone magnifier (such as the iPhone, a system magnifier, or ZoomText).

Here are some available magnifiers:

- Accessibar (Firefox extension) (*http://accessibar.mozdev.org/*)
- iPhone/iPod Touch/iPhoney (*http://www.apple.com/iphone/; http://source forge.net/projects/iphonesimulator/*)
- LowBrowse (Firefox add-on) (*https://addons.mozilla.org/en-US/firefox/ad don/8762*)
- MAGic (free demo version) (*http://www.freedomscientific.com/products/ lv/magic-bl-product-page.asp*)

- ZoomText (60-day free trial) (*http://www.aisquared.com/Products/Zoom TextMRD/index.cfm*)

Internet Explorer 8, Firefox 3, and Opera (all versions) have magnification built-in, as do Windows and Mac OS X. In Windows XP, look for it in Programs→Accessories→Accessibility→Magnifier. For Mac OS X, you'll find the "zoom" feature in System Preferences→Universal Access→Seeing.

Testing for mobile

The following tools can help you simulate the experience on a mobile device. As recommended by the dotMobi Web Developer's Guide, simulations and remote access services are useful ways to quickly catch obvious errors with markup or style sheets.

- Opera's "small screen view" (*http://www.opera.com/products/mobile/ smallscreen/*)
- Opera Mini Simulator (*http://www.operamini.com/demo/*)
- dotMobi emulator (choose between Sony K750 and Nokia N70) (*http:// mtld.mobi/emulator.php*)
- BlackBerry Simulators (*http://na.blackberry.com/eng/developers/down loads/simulators.jsp*)
- iPhoney (*http://sourceforge.net/projects/iphonesimulator/*)
- OpenWave Phone Simulator (*http://developer.openwave.com/dvl/tools _and_sdk/phone_simulator/*)
- DeviceAnywhere (*http://www.deviceanywhere.com/*)

After you've run your site or application through a few simulations and cleaned up the obvious issues, try it on an actual mobile device. Here is what the dotMobi Web Developer's Guide (page 72) says about that:

> If you have only one device, borrow phones from friends and family. Talk to vendors that may let you rent phones or use their device lab. If you don't have access to a vendor in your area, try going to a mobile service provider store and use the display phones for testing.

> Prepaid SIM cards from multiple mobile service provider networks can be a developer's best friend. Switching prepaid SIMs allows you to test on multiple devices across multiple networks, without having to commit to multiple contracts with mobile operators.

People

People should be an integral part of your development process both as resources to turn to when you have a question and as representatives of your audience. The following is a very meager sampling of the available forums:

- WAI Interest Group mailing list (*http://lists.w3.org/Archives/Public/w3c -wai-ig/*)
- WebAIM Accessibility E-mail Discussion List (*http://www.webaim.org/ discussion/*)
- Mozilla's dev-accessibility mailing list (*https://lists.mozilla.org/listinfo/dev -accessibility*)

As for usability testing, there are entire books about the subject. A great place to start is *Just Ask—Integrating Accessibility Throughout Design* by Shawn Lawton Henry. Henry outlines the user-centered design process, provides tips and tricks for including people with disabilities in user testing, and maintains a comprehensive list of resources. The book is available at *http://uiaccess.com/ accessucd/* for free.

20 Questions

Here is how to use the tools just listed to answer 20 questions about your site to help you gauge if you've followed the principles of universal design.

 These questions reflect most of the Level 1 Success Criteria in the Web Content Accessibility Guidelines 2.0 and a portion of the Mobile Web Best Practices. For a comprehensive list of Mobile Web Best Practices, refer to *http://www.w3.org/TR/ mobile-bp/*.

For the complete list of WCAG 2.0 Success Criteria and sufficient techniques, refer to the WCAG 2.0 Quick Reference (*http://www.w3.org/WAI/WCAG20/quickref/*).

To determine how these questions map to WCAG 2.0 Success Criteria and MWBP, refer to Table A-1 in the Appendix A.

Question 1. Text alternatives

Are text alternatives present and sufficiently equivalent to the graphic content? Audio-only content? Video-only content?

Inspect the list of images generated by the WAT (using Images→List images). Look for audio-only content (such as podcasts) and video-only content (such as webcams). Determine whether each of these has a text alternative. If it does,

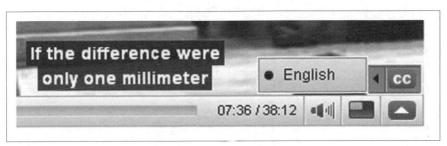

Figure 11-3. Turning on captions in YouTube

is the page/application usable with the text alternative only? If it isn't, what needs to be provided in text such that the page is usable?

Question 2. Multimedia

Is multimedia captioned? Does multimedia have audio descriptions or a full-text transcript?

Use the WAT to identify downloadable files or search the site or sections of the site where multimedia is likely to be. After you've found a file, watch part of the clip. If the clip has open captions, they will be displayed for everyone. If it uses closed captions, you'll need to turn on display of the captions. For YouTube videos, when the "full-screen" icon receives focus (either through a mouse hover or keyboard focus), if the clip has captions, a "cc" symbol pops up with a left arrow—as seen in Figure 11-3. Activating the left arrow shows a list of possible captioning files to choose from—usually a selection of languages.

Since most online media formats do not provide alternative audio tracks, audio descriptions are "open"—part of the primary audio track and available to everyone. Therefore, to test whether a clip has audio description, listen to part of it.

This article from AccessIT (an organization at the University of Washington) explains how to turn on captions and audio descriptions in Real Player, Windows Media, and Quicktime: *http://www.washington.edu/accessit/articles ?1251.*

Question 3. Link and control labels

Are controls (including links) appropriately identified or labeled?

This question ensures that controls (including Flash and Silverlight buttons, Ajax widgets, and HTML links and form elements) are all properly labeled. To test HTML links, use the WAT toolbar to create a link list (Doc info→List links). Look for image links that do not have alt text, links that are not

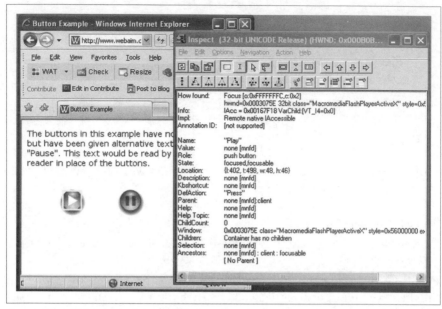

Figure 11-4. Using inspect32 to check the value of "name" on a Flash button

meaningful out of context, and duplicate links that go to different places. Also, note how many links are on a page and think about what that means for someone accessing the content via a mobile device or by the keyboard—alone or with a screen reader or screen magnifier. For example, *The New York Times* home page has 425 links. We'll return to this when we look at the structure of the page and how the links are grouped.

For Flash and Flex controls, use inspect32, shown in Figure 11-4, to ensure that the "name" value makes sense. For example, the "play" button is "play." (Try it yourself: *http://www.webaim.org/techniques/flash/media/button.html*.)

Use UISpy or Visual UIA Verifier to test whether Silverlight controls have a reasonable value for "name." For Ajax, use either inspect32 or AccProbe.

Question 4. Control groups

Are groups of controls appropriately identified?

Test that items grouped to form a control—such as options in a menu—are appropriately identified. In an Ajax menu, check that the menubar (usually the top-level div) is identified as such. You'll have to dig through the hierarchy (in inspect32 or AccProbe) to ensure that the current menu item's parent is properly identified, or you could look at the structure of the code (or DOM) to determine if the parent/child relationships make sense.

Question 5. Meaningful structure

Can a meaningful keyboard navigation order be derived from the document or application structure?

There are a variety of tools to inspect the structure of a page/application. Here are some options:

- Use a browser to tab through every link on the page.
- Use WAVE 4.0 for a visual representation for the reading order of a page. Select "Structure/Order View" from a WAVE report. The numbers indicate the order in which sections on the page will be read (if someone were to navigate by headings or divs).
- WAT Structure has 12 menu items related to structure, including headings, list items, and tab order. Tab order indicates the order in which links appear in the tab order (created by navigating a page by pressing only the Tab key).

 If you invoke one of these tests on a web application and receive the message "No active elements found," you're likely evaluating an Ajax application coded only with divs.

Things to keep in mind as you inspect the structure:

- Text that looks like a heading should be marked as a heading.
- Text that looks like a list should be marked as a list.
- Tab order shouldn't jump around the page; in general, the tab order should flow left-to-right and top-to-bottom, unless navigation links have specifically been placed at the end of the tab order, or unless you are using a left-to-right or vertical-based character set.

Question 6. Nonsensory operation

Can the document or application be operated when color, shape, size, location, or sound cannot be perceived?

The WAT has four tools to test color issues:

Greyscale
Removes all color from a page, except shades of grey.

Colour contrast analyzer
Selects a foreground color and a background color and tells you the contrast ratio for that combination. It even has an eyedropper so that you can grab colors from anything on the desktop.

Juicy Studio contrast analyzer
> Looks at all combinations of text on a page and determines for each: luminosity contrast ratio, difference in brightness, and difference in color. Each result is annotated with a "pass" or "fail" and how that differs for the three levels of WCAG 2.0.

Vischeck colorblindess simulator
> Simulates how someone with one of the three main colorblindess types (deuteranopia, protanopia, and tritanopia) might see your content.

As for testing, shape, size, and location, look for instructions in the content that refer to sensory characteristics of a control rather than referring to them by name. Examples of sensory-specific instructions include "use the green button" or "press the round button" or "press the top-left button."

Question 7. Automatic audio

> Can audio that plays automatically be stopped, paused, or silenced?

You'll have to load pages or change state in applications to determine if audio is triggered. If it is, ensure that it plays within a media control that allows the user to stop, pause, or lower the volume. Another option is to have audio silenced by default and provide an option for users to "click to hear audio" as is a recent trend with embedded advertising videos.

Question 8. Keyboard-only operation

> Can all functionality be operated via the keyboard alone?

Unplug your mouse. Use your app. Does it work? Pick a task that you expect people to perform when they visit your site. Can you do it—start to finish—without using a mouse?

Start a screen reader and turn off your monitor. As you interact with you application, are changes properly announced?

Question 9. Bypass blocks

> Is a skip navigation link present or are blocks of content identified such that they can be skipped?

Going back to the WAT tab order and heading structure reports, how many links are on a single page? How many navigation links appear in the tab order before the bulk of the content? Is a heading available at the beginning of each primary section of links or text? Even if you have a good structure, as the W3C WAI home page does, you still may want to provide a "Skip to main content" link or "Skip navigation."

This question is particularly relevant for sites that use menus at the top of each page. See Chapter 8 for a discussion about menus and tab order.

Assuming applications written in Silverlight or Flash or Flex have menus that act like system menus, this question is less relevant.

Question 10. Page titles

> Does each page in the site/application have a unique title that describes its topic or purpose?

Look at the name of the window as you access different pages. Check that the title changes when you open a new page.

Question 11. Language

> Is the human language identified for each page of the site/application?

Use WAT's "Doc Info→Show Lang Attributes." This works for any application embedded in an HTML page.

Question 12. Predictable behavior

> Is the application's behavior predictable in response to user input?

There are no tools that can test if something is predictable. If you have a control that looks like a system control, it should act like one. If you have a new control that doesn't look or act like anything else, schedule time to watch real people interact with it.

As we discuss in Chapter 8, there are some grey areas, one of which is menus created from lists of links. When in doubt, bring in people from your audience.

Question 13. Error identification and resolution

> Is it clear what information the user should provide? If the user makes an error, is the error clearly identified and suggestions provided for how to fix it?

Purposefully enter invalid values into your forms. Enter letters into number fields or use odd punctuation for a telephone number. What feedback does your form provide? Before someone enters any letters, is there any advice on what format is expected? When someone makes a mistake, what's the error message? Is it a generic "Fields marked with asterisks are required" or do you provide more information? In your error-checking code, can you tease out a variety of possible patterns to get the information you need?

Don't forget: avoid using only color to indicate fields that have errors (see Question 6).

Question 14. Syntactical and runtime errors

Have markup and programmatic syntax errors been fixed? Do XML-based languages validate? Do programmatic languages execute without error? Does it pass the MobileOK checker?

Run the W3C HTML and CSS validators.

At the moment, ARIA is not part of any HTML specification so you will receive validation errors. The goal is to incorporate ARIA into the HTML5 specification and at that time, the validation services will update to check for ARIA. In the meantime, people are working on tools to check ARIA syntax against the ARIA specification.

Run scripts to ensure no runtime errors occur or if they do, that they degrade gracefully.

Run MobileOK.

Question 15. Change notification

Does the site or application use accessibility features or APIs (such as ARIA, UIA, and MSAA) such that user agents including assistive technologies are notified of changes to all user interface components?

This is primarily an issue for custom controls, including Ajax. Implementing ARIA is key to answering "yes" for an Ajax application. If your Silverlight and Flash/Flex applications use base classes, this information should also be provided as part of the core class library. You'll definitely want to test custom components, even if they extend core classes.

Listen to the feedback provided by NVDA, Jaws10, or FireVox as you run other tests, especially keyboard-only operation. You'll want to hear something announced for every user action, particularly those that cause the application to execute a function or change the visual display.

Question 16. Timed response

If a page requires a timed response, can someone turn off, adjust, or extend the time limit? (See exceptions.)

Think about the various tasks on your site or application. Do any of them time out? If users needs more time, what do they do? If they are not given more time, what happens?

There are some exceptions:

- The time limit is a required part of a real-time event, and no alternative to the time limit is possible.
- The time limit is essential and extending it would invalidate the activity.
- The time limit is longer than 20 hours.

This means that auctions do not need to provide more time.

Question 17. Moving, blinking, and scrolling

> If a site/application has moving, blinking, or scrolling information, is there a way for a person to pause, stop, or hide the content? (See exceptions.)

This question hangs on from the days of <blink> and <marquee>. Thankfully, those elements are deprecated. However, people can create similar effects with scripts, so it is still an issue. Ads are also designed to be distracting, and while this is great for business, it can prevent people from focusing on the main content of a page or application. If it is not possible to provide a mechanism to pause, stop, or hide distracting content, another option is to avoid the infinite loop—play distracting content only once.

Testing this is a matter of finding distracting content and then trying to pause, stop, or hide it.

Question 18. Auto-update

> If a site/application auto-updates, is there a way for a person to control the frequency of updates? (See exceptions.)

This is related to Question 15. The first thing is that a person needs to know when the page updates. If it is updating too quickly, a person needs to pause, stop, or hide the updating content.

Question 19. Flashing content

> Does the page avoid anything that flashes more than three times per second? (See general flash and red flash thresholds.)

The tests are fairly complicated. In this case, please refer to the Web Content Accessibility Guidelines 2.0 Quick Reference information at *http://www.w3.org/WAI/WCAG20/quickref/#seizure*.

You'll want to download the Photosensitive Epilepsy Analysis Tool (PEAT) available from at *http://trace.wisc.edu/peat/*.

Question 20. Field testing

> Has the site/application been tested with a variety of browsers, mobile devices, and assistive technologies? Have you watched real people use the site or application? Is it possible to accomplish a complete process (e.g., search for a product, add it to a shopping cart, and check out)?

Refer to the list of browsers, mobile simulators, and assistive technologies in the previous section.

Team Structures and Strategies

Organizations that produce web content come in all shapes and sizes, but in all but the most oppressive of environments, the practice of universal design can make itself known. Here are some common patterns we've come across and the strategies necessary to make UD successful within them.

The one-person team

We've discussed how UD is a shared responsibility. But obviously, it has to start somewhere, even in units of one.

If your web operation consists of just you—you're the author, designer, and developer—your chief responsibility is to police yourself. That means making changes to your own content production process to minimize the amount of work you have to do to maintain accessibility as you go. It's up to you how to make the process work, but you should constantly be paying attention to how you go about your business, looking for ways to optimize. You may find, for example, that creating templates as you go preserves the metadata you need, but you have to do by hand each time.

This may seem like overkill when it's only you who's working with it. But developing the discipline necessary to design inclusively does scale, and when you find yourself in an organization where the jobs are split up, you will be able to point out who needs to be doing what.

Small teams

Once the "webmaster" becomes a "web team," some clear roles emerge. You may have a designer or two, a developer or two, maybe a project manager to keep everything running smoothly. Most often, these people will be in support of others—internal resources such as a marketing department, or perhaps a client—whose only functions are to write copy, or launch new sites or subsites.

At this scale, it's easy to lose direction. Marketing may jump in and say, "Drop everything. We've got this new campaign, and you're doing the web design for it." Or the client may ask for something with more "pop" or "zing," without the technical know-how to even name it. Make it more like Gmail, they'll say. Or Facebook. No! *Twitter!*

In this environment, your job is to ensure that the inmates don't end up running the asylum. What you know is that the people on your team can either enable you, or they have the power to undo all of your work. Be clear with everyone who can touch your code that you have done certain things for a reason; watch for people who impede your progress, and find out why. If they simply don't understand the principles involved, sit them down to explain the situation, and work with them so that they have the skills necessary to complement your work. (For advice on people who are getting in the way on purpose, read on.)

It is important to act as a resource for UD issues and problems and not as the "accessibility police." If you can show your work's benefits, people feel more confident in working toward the common goal, and think more creatively about reaching it. This kind of culture won't grow if you try to lay down the law, issuing policies and banning this or that. The goal is to make it easier to do more things right than wrong. This is called *enlightened self-interest*, and when it clicks within an organization, it's like magic.

Larger teams

Companies made up of several dozen up to a couple hundred web professionals have an opportunity to establish an end-to-end strategy for universal design. What is essential in this environment is to sell it well.

Large web companies and consultancies generally work in groups made up of designers, frontend and backend developers, testers, and copywriters, often sprinkled with project managers, account managers, and company-wide support staff (tech support, database admins, etc.). To effect change in an organization of this size, the best approach is to show your fellow team members that universal design is going to save them a lot of time—and if they are all singing from the same hymn sheet, it will.

Once that's achieved, and you have a group doing better, more efficient work, you have a chance to leave your mark on the whole organization's culture. Point out weak spots in how you approach projects, how you prototype, what tools you recommend to clients, and so on. Challenge other teams to develop more universal products with each launch. A team that produces a one-off site that exhibits great UD practices is nothing next to a team that improves on its work with every single product it develops.

Big organizations and free-for-alls

We worked for several years at the W3C, an organization made up entirely of people who can handcode valid, semantic HTML in their sleep. An organization with this degree of distributed knowledge about web authoring processes has different problems from the average corporation. The head of communications at the time, Janet Daly, talked about having "70 employees, 70 webmasters"—in a manner that made it very clear that this is not always a good thing.

Design agencies are a perfect example of what can go wrong. Let's say a client hires you to do ongoing work on a corporate site. As the leader of the redesign, you carefully build your site using solid universal design practices: clean code, simple content, reasonable affordances for mobile and assistive technology users. At the end, you hand off your code to other designers, either from your agency or your client.

Then a few months later, you return to find that the site has fallen apart in your absence. Numerous slapdash modifications have been made, destroying the work you've done to improve the overall interaction design of the site.

This is a very common side effect called *site decay*. It happens when the design expertise and/or understanding of the site's goals are unevenly distributed. There are many sources of site decay:

- Work is being assigned to less-skilled workers or third-party consultants; for example, a site is going from active development into maintenance mode, and more junior developers are taking over.
- Maintenance information has not been adequately documented and handed off.
- New features have been added that either fail to adopt or actively interfere with the site's existing UD practices.
- UD has ceased to be a priority in the ongoing design work.

Regardless of the source, the outcome can be frustrating. Experiencing this phenomenon over and over again may explain the often-sour dispositions of many long-time specialists in accessibility (not to mention usability, internationalization, security...). It's hard being an Iron Chef when you're surrounded by "Boyardees."

Those of us who don't write the checks can't expect that everyone working on a site will have the same level of skill, not to mention the discipline to do all the work that's necessary. You can, however, set yourself up for success by specifying how content is passed from one person to the next, and expressing expectations that UD techniques won't be stripped out or disabled by the next person in the process.

Cross-Reference for Universal Design for Web Applications

These 20 questions are based on the Level A Success Criteria in the November 3, 2008 Proposed Recommendation of WCAG 2.0. They do not directly map to the WCAG 2.0 Success Criteria and may generalize advice given in WCAG 2.0 . As such, the ultimate reference for WCAG 2.0 is the current version of WCAG 2.0, available at *http://www.w3.org/TR/WCAG20/*.

The WAI's Education and Outreach Working Group has collaborated with the Mobile Web Best Practices Working Group on a series of resources called "Web Content Accessibility and Mobile Web: Making a Web Site Accessible Both for People with Disabilities and for Mobile Devices," which include mappings between WCAG 2.0 and MWBP 1.0.

Table A-1 is our interpretation of the mapping. Please refer to the WAI Education and Outreach Working Group (EOWG) resources if there is a discrepancy (*http://www.w3.org/WAI/mobile/*).

Table A-1. Mapping between accessibility and mobile specifications and Universal Design for Web Applications (UD4WA)

Question	WCAG 2.0 Ref	MWBP Ref	UD4WA Ref
1. Are text alternatives present and sufficiently equivalent to the graphic content? Audio-only content? Video-only content?	**1.1.1 Non-text Content:** All non-text content that is presented to the user has a text alternative that serves the equivalent purpose, except for the situations listed below. **1.2.1 Audio-only and Video-only (Prerecorded):** For prerecorded audio-only and prerecorded video-only media, the following are true, except when the audio or video is a media alternative for text and is clearly labeled as such: • Prerecorded Audio-only: A text alternative is provided that presents equivalent information for prerecorded audio-only content. • Prerecorded Video-only: Either a text alternative or an audio track is provided that presents equivalent information for prerecorded video-only content.	**5.4.5 Non-Text Items [NON-TEXT_ALTERNATIVES]** Provide a text equivalent for every non-text element.	Metadata, Images. Video and Audio, Transcripts and Text Alternatives.
2. Is multimedia captioned? Does multimedia have audio descriptions or a full-text transcript?	**1.2.2 Captions (Prerecorded):** Captions are provided for all prerecorded audio content in synchronized media, except when the media is a media alternative for text and is clearly labeled as such. **1.2.3 Audio Description or Full Text Alternative:** A full text alternative for synchronized media, including any interaction or audio description of the prerecorded video content, is provided for synchronized media, except when the media is a media alternative for text and is clearly labeled as such.		Video and Audio, Captioning your video. Video and Audio, Audio Description. Video and Audio, Transcripts and Text Alternatives.
3. Are controls (including links) appropriately identified or labeled?	**1.3.1 Info and Relationships:** Information, structure, and relationships conveyed through presentation can be programmatically determined or are available in text.	**5.2.6 Link Target Identification [LINK_TARGET_ID]** Clearly identify the target of each link.	Metadata, Link text. Forms, Labels.

Question	WCAG 2.0 Ref	MWBP Ref	UD4WA Ref
	2.4.4 Link Purpose (In Context): The purpose of each link can be determined from the link text alone, or from the link text together with its programmatically determined link context, except where the purpose of the link would be ambiguous to users in general.	**5.5.3 Labels for Form Controls [CONTROL_LABELLING]** Label all form controls appropriately and explicitly associate labels with form controls.	Scripting, Throughout. Ajax/ARIA, Throughout.
	4.1.2 Name, Role, Value: For all user interface components (including but not limited to: form elements, links, and components generated by scripts), the name and role can be programmatically determined; states, properties, and values that can be set by the user can be programmatically set; and notification of changes to these items is available to user agents, including assistive technologies.	**5.5.3 Labels for Form Controls [CONTROL_PO-SITION]** Position labels so they lay out properly in relation to the form controls they refer to.	RIAs, Throughout.
4. Are groups of controls appropriately identified?	**1.3.1 Info and Relationships:** Information, structure, and relationships conveyed through presentation can be programmatically determined or are available in text.	**5.5.3 Labels for Form Controls [CONTROL_LABELLING]** Label all form controls appropriately and explicitly associate labels with form controls. **5.5.3 Labels for Form Controls [CONTROL_PO-SITION]** Position labels so they lay out properly in relation to the form controls they refer to.	Forms, Labels.
5. Can a meaningful keyboard navigation order be derived from the document or application structure?	**1.3.1 Info and Relationships:** Information, structure, and relationships conveyed through presentation can be programmatically determined or are available in text. **1.3.2 Meaningful Sequence:** When the sequence in which content is presented affects its meaning, a correct reading sequence can be programmatically determined. **2.4.3 Focus Order:** If a Web page can be navigated sequentially and the navigation sequences affect meaning or operation, focusable com-	**5.5.2 Tab Order [TAB_ORDER]** Create a logical order through links, form controls, and objects. MWBP says to avoid using tables "unless the device is known to support them." And, where possible, use an alternative to tables.	Forms, Tab order. Tables, Multiple sections. Scripting, Multiple sections. Process, 20 Questions.

Question	WCAG 2.0 Ref	MWBP Ref	UD4WA Ref
	ponents receive focus in an order that preserves meaning and operability.		
6. Can the document or application be operated when color, shape, size, location, or sound cannot be perceived?	1.3.3 Sensory Characteristics: Instructions provided for understanding and operating content do not rely solely on sensory characteristics of components such as shape, size, visual location, orientation, or sound.	5.3.6 Color [USE_OF_COLOR] Ensure that information conveyed with color is also available without color.	Process, 20 Questions. Structure and Design, Color.
	1.4.1 Use of Color: Color is not used as the only visual means of conveying information, indicating an action, prompting a response, or distinguishing a visual element.		
7. Can audio that plays automatically be stopped, paused, or silenced?	1.4.2 Audio Control: If any audio on a web page plays automatically for more than three seconds, either a mechanism is available to pause or stop the audio, or a mechanism is available to control audio volume independently from the overall system volume level.	5.4.5 Non-Text Items [OBJECTS_OR_SCRIPT] Do not rely on embedded objects or script.	Process, 20 Questions.
8. Can all functionality be operated via the keyboard alone?	2.1.1 Keyboard: All functionality of the content is operable through a keyboard interface without requiring specific timings for individual keystrokes, except where the underlying function requires input that depends on the path of the user's movement and not just the endpoints.	5.4.5 Non-Text Items [OBJECTS_OR_SCRIPT] Do not rely on embedded objects or script.	Scripting, Throughout the chapter.
	2.1.2 No Keyboard Trap: If keyboard focus can be moved to a component of the page using a keyboard interface, then focus can be moved away from that component using only a keyboard interface, and, if it requires more than unmodified arrow or Tab keys, the user is advised of the method for moving focus away.		
9. Is a skip navigation link present or are blocks of content identified such that they can be skipped?	2.4.1 Bypass Blocks: A mechanism is available to bypass blocks of content that are repeated on multiple web pages.	5.2.2 Navigation Bar [NAVBAR] Provide only minimal navigation at the top of the page.	Metadata, Language and character encoding.

Question	WCAG 2.0 Ref	MWBP Ref	UD4WA Ref
10. Does each page in the site/application have a unique title that describes its topic or purpose?	2.4.2 Page Titled: Web pages have titles that describe topic or purpose.	5.2.5 Access Keys [ACCESS_KEYS] Assign access keys to links in navigational menus and frequently accessed functionality. 5.4.3 Structural Elements [STRUCTURE] Use features of the markup language to indicate logical document structure. 5.4.1 Title [PAGE_TITLE] Provide a short but descriptive page title.	Metadata, Titles.
11. Is the human language identified for each page of the site/application?	3.1.1 Language of Page: The default human language of each web page can be programmatically determined.	5.4.12 Character Encoding [CHARACTER_ENCODING_USE] Indicate in the response the character encoding being used.	Metadata, Language and character encoding.
12. Is the application's behavior predictable in response to user input?	3.2.1 On Focus: When any component receives focus, it does not initiate a change of context. 3.2.2 On Input: Changing the setting of any user interface component does not automatically cause a change of context unless the user has been advised of the behavior before using the component.	5.4.5 Non-Text Items [OBJECTS_OR_SCRIPT] Do not rely on embedded objects or script.	Process, 20 Questions.
13. Is it clear what information the user should provide? If the user makes an error, is the error clearly identified and suggestions provided for how to fix it?	3.3.1 Error Identification: If an input error is automatically detected, the item that is in error is identified and the error is described to the user in text. 3.3.2 Labels or Instructions: Labels or instructions are provided when content requires user input.	5.5.1 Input [MINIMIZE_KEYSTROKES] Keep the number of keystrokes to a minimum. 5.5.1 Input [AVOID_FREE_TEXT] Avoid free-text entry where possible. 5.5.1 Input [PROVIDE_DEFAULTS] Provide preselected default values where possible.	Forms, Error handling. WCAG 2.0 focuses on error identification and user recovery; MWBP seems to take

Question	WCAG 2.0 Ref	MWBP Ref	UD4WA Ref
		5.5.1 Input [DEFAULT_INPUT_MODE] Specify a default text entry mode, language, and/or input format, if the device is known to support it.	the approach of preventing user errors.
14. Have markup and programmatic syntax errors been fixed? Do XML-based languages validate? Do programmatic languages execute without error? Does it pass the MobileOK checker?	4.1.1 Parsing: In content implemented using markup languages, elements have complete start and end tags, elements are nested according to their specifications, elements do not contain duplicate attributes, and any IDs are unique, except where the specifications allow these features.	5.4.7 Valid Markup [VALID_MARKUP] Create documents that validate to published formal grammars.	Process, Evaluation Tools and Resources, 20 Questions.
15. Does the site or application use accessibility features or APIs (such as ARIA, UIA, and MSAA) such that user agents, including assistive technologies, are notified of changes to all user interface components?	4.1.2 Name, Role, Value: For all user interface components (including but not limited to: form elements, links and components generated by scripts), the name and role can be programmatically determined; states, properties, and values that can be set by the user can be programmatically set; and notification of changes to these items is available to user agents, including assistive technologies.	5.5.3 Labels for Form Controls [CONTROL_LABELLING] Label all form controls appropriately and explicitly associate labels with form controls. 5.4.5 Non-Text Items [OBJECTS_OR_SCRIPT] Do not rely on embedded objects or script.	Scripting, Throughout. Ajax/ARIA, Throughout. RIAs, Throughout.
16. If a page requires a timed response, can someone turn off, adjust, or extend the time limit? (See exceptions.)	2.2.1 Timing Adjustable: For each time limit that is set by the content, at least one of the following is true: • Turn off: The user is allowed to turn off the time limit before encountering it; or • Adjust: The user is allowed to adjust the time limit before encountering it over a wide range that is at least 10 times the length of the default setting; or • Extend: The user is warned before time expires and given at least 20 seconds to extend the time limit with a simple action (for		Process, 20 Questions.

Question	WCAG 2.0 Ref	MWBP Ref	UD4WA Ref
	example, "press the Space bar"), and the user is allowed to extend the time limit at least 10 times; or		
	• Real-time Exception: The time limit is a required part of a real-time event (for example, an auction), and no alternative to the time limit is possible; or		
	• Essential Exception: The time limit is essential and extending it would invalidate the activity; or		
	• 20-Hour Exception: The time limit is longer than 20 hours.		
17. If a site/application has moving, blinking, or scrolling information, is there a way for a person to pause, stop, or hide the content? (See exceptions.)	2.2.2 Moving, blinking, scrolling: For any moving, blinking or scrolling information that (1) starts automatically, (2) lasts more than five seconds, and (3) is presented in parallel with other content, there is a mechanism for the user to pause, stop, or hide it unless the movement, blinking, or scrolling is part of an activity where it is essential.	5.4.3 Structural Elements [STRUCTURE] Use features of the markup language to indicate logical document structure. 5.4.16 Fonts [FONTS] Do not rely on support of font-related styling. 5.4.5 Non-Text Items [OBJECTS_OR_SCRIPT] Do not rely on embedded objects or script.	Process, 20 Questions.
18. If a site/application auto-updates, is there a way for a person to control the frequency of updates? (See exceptions.)	2.2.2 Auto-updating: For any auto-updating information that (1) starts automatically, (2) lasts more than five seconds, and (3) is presented in parallel with other content, there is a mechanism for the user to pause, stop, or hide it or to control the frequency of the update unless the auto-updating is part of an activity where it is essential.	5.2.8 Refreshing, Redirection and Spawned Windows [AUTO_REFRESH] Do not create periodically auto-refreshing pages, unless you have informed the user and provided a means of stopping it.	Process, 20 Questions.
19. Does the page avoid anything that flashes more than three times per second? (See general flash and red flash thresholds.)	2.3.1 Three Flashes or Below Threshold: Web pages do not contain anything that flashes more than three times in any one-second period, or the flash is below the general flash and red flash thresholds.		Structure and Design, Flicker and patterns.

Question	WCAG 2.0 Ref	MWBP Ref	UD4WA Ref
20. Has the site/application been tested with a variety of browsers, mobile devices, and assistive technologies? Have you watched real people use the site or application? Is it possible to accomplish a complete process (e.g., search for a product, add it to a shopping cart, and check out)?		**5.1.4 Testing [TESTING]** Carry out testing on actual devices as well as emulators.	Process, Throughout.

Index

A

abbr element, title attribute, 74
absolute length units, 43
Accerciser, 146
accessibility, 10
    audience for web application content, 11
    considered early and throughout design process, 21
    direct accessibility with WAI-ARIA, 110
    evaluation tools and resources, 144–150
    growth opportunity offered by aging population, 13
    industry standards related to, 17
    mapping between mobile specifications and UD4WA, 163
    Microsoft tools for testing, 136
    primary issues with web applications, 32
    showing and hiding content, 93–105
    software accessibility, 125
    testing for, 136
    training in and maintenance of practices, 144
    in video, 81–88
accessibility APIs, 128
accessible design, 3
Accessible Rich Internet Applications (see ARIA; WAI-ARIA)
accesskey attribute, 54

AccProbe tool, 137, 146
ACTF (Accessibility Tools Framework), 137
ActionScript, 128
active elements, using :hover with, 94
addresses (billing and shipping), organizing separately, 53
aDesigner tool, 137
Adobe
    Flash Player 9, working with Flex on Internet Tablets, 127
    Phostshop CS4 and Illustrator CS4, accessibility testing tool, 138
    RIAs and Flex platform, 126
aging population, increased need for accessibility, 13
Ajax, 91, 107–123
    (see also ARIA)
    process or mindset for designing applications, 111
    support in assistive technology, 109
    support in web browsers, 108
    taking stock of existing code, 108
alt attribute, HTML img element, 24
Americans with Disabilities Act of 1990, 15
Android mobile platform, 5
Apple, NSAccessibility API, 128
architecture, 2
ARIA (Accessible Rich Internet Application), 107–123
    bridge between web and software accessibility, 110
    disabling controls, 122

We'd like to hear your suggestions for improving our indexes. Send email to *index@oreilly.com*.

error handling in form data validation, 121

handling updates, 118

maintaining relationships among DOM nodes, 123

navigation and keyboard support, 114–118

pointing from control to its label and description, 120

roles, 112

setting reading order with aria-flowto, 119

states and properties, 113

support for, 110

tabindex, 103

WAI-ARIA standard, 93

ARIA (Accessible Rich Internet Applications), 18

aria-controls attribute, 119

aria-describedby attribute, 120

aria-expanded property, 114

aria-flowto attribute, 119

aria-haspopup property, 114

aria-labelled by attribute, 120

aria-live property, 118

aria-owns attribute, 123

assistive technology

open source, support for ARIA, 110

support for Ajax, 109

support for RIAs, 127

ATAG (Authoring Tool Accessibility Guidelines), 18, 141

CMSs (content management systems), 142

Version 2.0, xii

ATAG 2.0 (Authoring Tool Accessibility Guidelines 2.0)

prompting users to generate accessible code, 136

audio descriptions, adding to video, 86

audio, transcripts of, 88

authoring tools, 18

AxsJAX, 110

B

bandwidth requirements, video, 80

borders in data tables, 75

C

CAPTCHA, 25, 63

text alternatives for images, 29

captioning, 81

captioning your video, 83

formats, 83

hiring a captioner, 85

video on mobile devices, 87

captions, 82

for data tables, 68

character encodings, 31

Chen, Charles, 110

Chrome browser, 5

class attribute, 37

client side form validation, 61

closed captioning, 81

Closed Captioning website, 86

CMSs (content management systems), 141

code examples from this book, xiv

code, taking stock of existing code, 108

codecs, 78

color

flashing content, 47

issues with use in web applications, 41

use in mobile device video captions, 87

use in tabular data, 74

color contrast, 42

color differentiation, 41

colorblindness, 41

column widths, 75

community contributions, 143

Completely Automated Public Turing Tests to Tell Computers and Humans Apart (see CAPTCHA)

complex data tables, 69

specifying relationships between data and headings, 71

summaries, 70

content management systems (CMSs), 141

controls, disabling, 122

CPU usage by video, 80

CSS (Cascading Style Sheets), 35, 42–46

focus, managing for keyboard handlers, 118
font element, 37
fonts
    mobile device video captions, 87
    Web fonts, 45
footnotes for tables, 74
for attribute, label element, 52
formatting issues in form data, 62
forms, 51–65
    accesskey attribute, 54
    CAPTCHAs, 63
    descriptions of controls, 121
    error handling in data validation, 121
    fieldset and legend elements, 52
    labels, 52
    tab order, 56
    validation of data, 60
        client side, 61
        server side, 63

G

GET and POST methods, 36
Google
    Android mobile platform, 5
    AxsJAX scripts injecting pages with ARIA properties, 110
    disabilities as a user, 14
    Webmaster Guidelines on textual alternatives to images, 25
Google Video, captioning support, 82
graceful degradation, 108
graphs, text describing, 28

H

H.264 codec, 79
HD (high definition) video, 79
headings, 38
    relationships between data and, 71
    table cells, 68
hearing disabilities, 88
Henry, Shawn, 21
hiding content, 95
    using display:none to hide submenus, 99
:hover pseudoselector

highlighting items not receiving focus in CSS, 104
    use with active elements, issues with, 94–101
    using with inactive elements, 101
HTML
    accesskey attribute, 54
    designing for email, 48
    document-based origins as application framework, 35
    limitations of, 91
    roles and states for controls, 109
    roles and states of controls defined in ARIA, 110
    semantics, 37
    tabindex attribute, 58
html element, lang attribute, 31

I

IAccessible interface, 128
IAccessible2 interface, 128
id attribute, 37
Illustrator CS4, accessibility testing tool, 138
images, 24
    dimensions of, 29
    of text, 44
    text alternatives for, 135
    use in CSS, 44
    writing guidelines for text alternatives, 25
inactive elements, using :hover with, 101
inspect32 accessibility testing tool, 136
international situational disabilities, 12
Internet-connected devices, non-PC, 5
iPhone, 4
    difficulties with using, 10
    forms, optimization of, 53
iTunes, support for high definition video, 79

J

Java accessibility, 126
JavaScript, 92
    alert boxes for errors in form data, 62
    element.focus( ), 103
    event handlers, 104

About the Authors

Wendy Chisholm is a consultant, developer, author, and speaker on the topic of universal design. As coeditor of the Web Content Accessibility Guidelines 1.0 (WCAG 1.0) and then a staff member at the World Wide Web Consortium, she has worked with people around the globe to make the Web accessible. Currently residing in Seattle, WA, Wendy consults with market leaders such as Microsoft, Adobe, and Google, integrating universal design concepts into their tools and technologies. She continues to further the research and development of universal design as a part-time staff member at the University of Washington.

Matt May is a developer, technologist, and accessibility advocate responsible for working internally and externally with Adobe product teams and customers to address accessibility in Adobe products, ensure interoperability with assistive technologies, and make customers aware of the many accessibility features that already exist in Adobe products.

Prior to joining Adobe, Matt worked for W3C/WAI on many of the core standards in web accessibility; led the Web Standards Project's Accessibility Task Force; helped to architect one of the first online grocery sites, Home-Grocer.com; and co-founded Blue Flavor, a respected web and mobile design consultancy.

Colophon

The animal on the cover of *Universal Design for Web Applications* is an Italian greyhound, the smallest of the family of gazehounds (sighthounds). Believed to originate more than 2,000 years ago in the Mediterranean basin, Italian greyhounds are sleek, active toy dogs that stand approximately 12–15 inches tall and weigh 7–11 pounds. Often referred to as a miniature greyhound, the Italian greyhound shares many characteristics with its larger cousin, including a tucked-in abdomen, an arched back, and a fine, silky coat in shades of gray, cream, red, fawn, brown, black, or brindle.

The dog's affectionate and gentle temperament makes it a popular pet today; its extremely short, odorless coat makes it a good option for people with allergies or other pet sensitivities. It is an intelligent and loyal companion. Though it does not require as much exercise as larger breeds and can be quite happy as an apartment dog, an Italian greyhound should have regular walks and light play sessions. It may refuse to go outside if it is raining or too cold for its short hair and small stature, so some owners have successfully litter-trained their Italian greyhounds.

A favorite with Italians of the 16th century (a fact which gives the breed its name), Italian greyhounds were among the many miniature dogs in high demand at the time. They are featured in Renaissance paintings by prominent artists such as Carpaccio, Van der Weyden, and Bosch. The dogs have also been popular with royal families throughout history, including England's James I, Catherine the Great, and Queen Victoria. In the mid-1800s, an Italian greyhound became America's "first pet" when President John Tyler bought his wife a puppy they named "Le Beau."

The cover image is from Cassell's Natural History. The cover font is Adobe ITC Garamond. The text font is Linotype Birka; the heading font is Adobe Myriad Condensed; and the code font is LucasFont's TheSansMonoCondensed.

Related Titles from O'Reilly

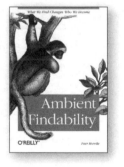

Web Programming

ActionScript 3.0 Cookbook

ActionScript 3.0 Design Patterns

ActionScript for Flash MX: The Definitive Guide, *2nd Edition*

Advanced Rails

AIR for JavaScript Developer's Pocket Guide

Ajax Design Patterns

Ajax Hacks

Ajax on Rails

Ajax: The Definitive Guide

Building Scalable Web Sites

Designing Web Navigation

Dynamic HTML: The Definitive Reference, *3rd Edition*

Essential ActionScript 3.0

Essential PHP Security

Flash Hacks

Head First HTML with CSS & XHTML

Head Rush Ajax

High Performance Web Sites

HTTP: The Definitive Guide

JavaScript & DHTML Cookbook, *2nd Edition*

JavaScript Pocket Reference, *2nd Edition*

JavaScript: The Definitive Guide, *5th Edition*

Learning ActionScript 3.0

Learning PHP and MySQL, *2nd Edition*

PHP Cookbook, *2nd Edition*

PHP Hacks

PHP in a Nutshell

PHP Pocket Reference, *2nd Edition*

PHP Unit Pocket Guide

Programming ColdFusion MX, *2nd Edition*

Programming Flex 2

Programming PHP, *2nd Edition*

Programming Rails

Rails Cookbook

Upgrading to PHP 5

Web Database Applications with PHP and MySQL, *2nd Edition*

Web Scripting Power Tools

Web Site Cookbook

Webmaster in a Nutshell, *3rd Edition*

O'REILLY®

Our books are available at most retail and online bookstores.

To order direct: 1-800-998-9938 • *order@oreilly.com* • *www.oreilly.com*

Online editions of most O'Reilly titles are available by subscription at *safari.oreilly.com*